Other books by Dirk Wales:

*A Lucky Dog, the Story of Owney,
1890's U.S. Rail Mail Mascot*

*The Further Adventures of A Lucky Dog,
1890's U.S. Rail Mail Mascot*

Jack London's Dog

Penny House

*Twice a Hero: Heroes of the
American Revolutionary War*

Shadow Angel

The Giraffe Who Walked to Paris

ABANDONED Z
A journey from Z to A

Best Wishes

Dirk Wales

Scrap Metal Alphabet by Mark Winter

GREAT PLAINS PRESS

Great Plains Press
1103 Canyon Road
Santa Fe, New Mexico 87501

nancy@greatplainspress.com

©2015 Dirk Wales

Book Design and Photography by Townsend Artman
Jacket Design by Lucy Morrison

Thanks To:

Charlie, Doreen, Matt, Ryan, and Don at Forrest Auto for use of their company yard for location photography.

Karl and Mary Jane Blaha for use of their metal salvage trailer for additional location photography.

This book is dedicated to
Susan Murphy-Milano
who has been a constant inspiration.

The first letter he placed on top of the junk pile was **Z**. No one could see the Z, but Zane didn't know that.

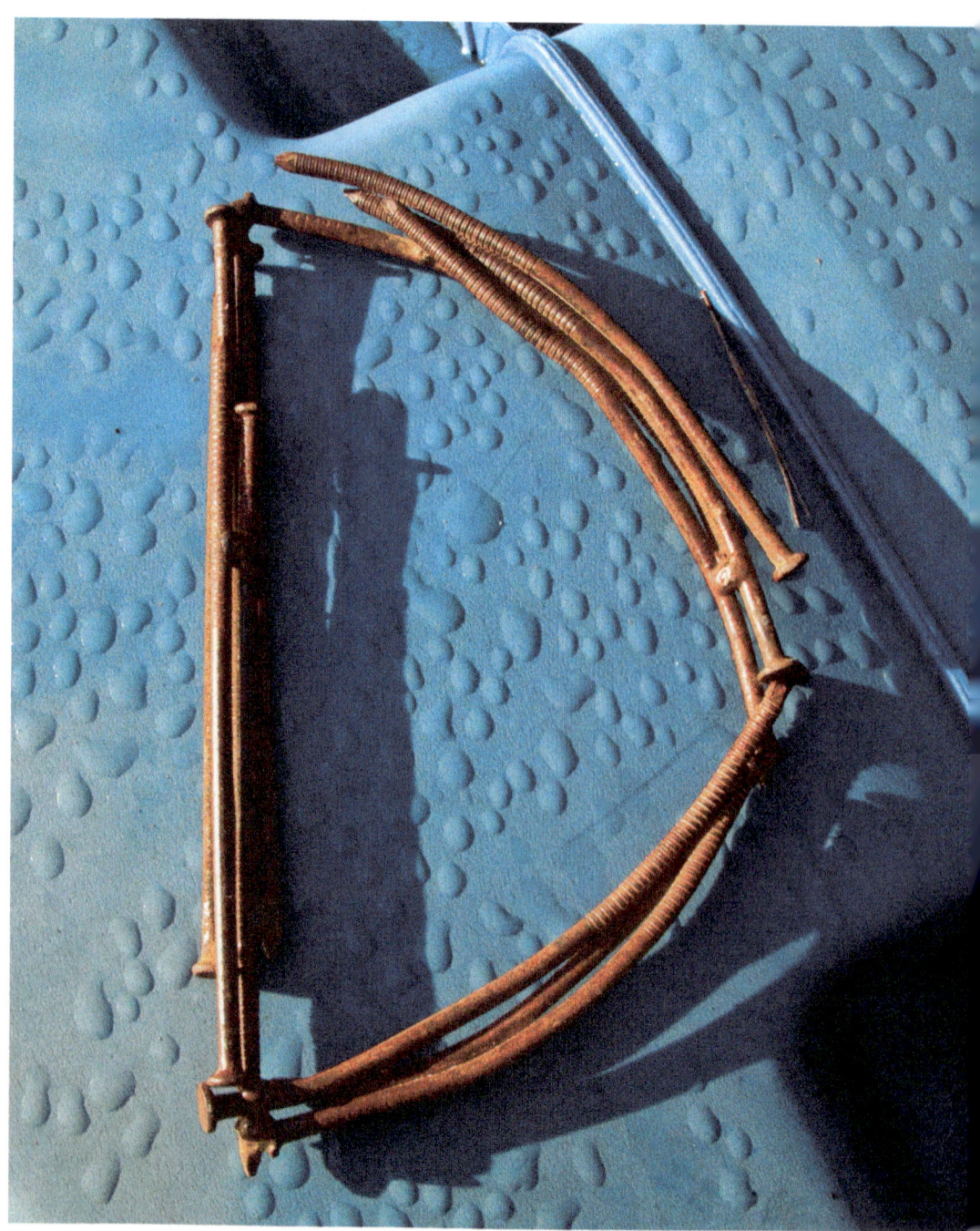

2

D was nails Zane had glued together.

That's all he was now, the two letters of his name: Z D.

Right over them was **E**. This letter had the most meaning for Zane.

He made the E with two pairs of broken scissors. He was careful not to cut himself as he e pox ied them together. But, that's the way he felt anyway.

Cut.

Now, Zane had three letters on top of the junk mountain in the middle of the junkyard, but he didn't know they couldn't be seen by the outside world yet. They weren't quite high enough.

Zane hadn't realized his idea for getting some attention for the junkyard from the town around him would be so much fun. It had lifted his spirits until he stepped back to see the ugly cutting E he had made…then he was sad again. He picked up a broken mirror by his foot and looked at himself. Just a plain 16 year old kid.

Zane Dancer — Z D — was a kid who wanted to be creative, do fun stuff, but he had been abandoned by his family who ran the junkyard for the town. His mother, who loved Zane, had to leave with Zane's father who was in charge of the junkyard… and was not-a-very-nice-man. Lots of times the father had yelled at Zane and his Mom, and sometimes had hit Zane. And, he had hurt Zane's mother. He was just not a good father for a creative and sensitive kid, or for his family.

So now, Zane was going to use his creative idea to build a tower of letters to spell a word — a b a n d o n d e d Z — he wanted the world and his small town to know that he had to add "abandoned" to how he felt and how he missed his folks. But, if they really loved him, why had they left? That's what he didn't understand.

So, now he was on his own — and if he understood why he was left on his own, it might help him to know what to do. So, now he would do the only thing that seemed to be "next" to him — the tower of letters.

Fortunately, he had his dog, Moxie, and he had found the big box of epoxy. "What is it?" his mom had asked when he first brought it home.

Zane read the label to her: *E pox yie*. It's glue, Mom.

Throw it away, his father had said.

No, said Zane, I might need it for something.

Dumb kid, his father had said. But all this happened awhile ago, before they had left Zane alone in the junkyard. Zane had known way back then that the *e pox yie* was going to be important someday. Like Today.

Zane walked in circles around the junkyard with Moxie right beside him, wondering. Why did they leave? Would they come back? What is this about? And mainly, what should he do now? Should he start attending school regularly instead of now and then, which he had been doing and not doing? Who would take care of the junkyard? Moxie could sense Zane's distress and followed him closely in circles around the junkyard.

Zane had not paid much attention to the small "sculptures" he had made over the years, but now he really noticed them. The most fun was the one he had made from an old toolbox someone had left. He had taken his epoxy and made a small upward-moving tower of tools. At the base to hold them down was the toolbox. Then one by one he had connected all of the tools in an upward tower – the hammer, the pliers, the screwdrivers, seven of them, the hacksaw, and finally on top, the wrench, open and ready. Even his father had liked that sculpture. But the one his mother liked best – where was that one? He walked around turning things over until he found it.

A stack of clothing irons.

He had collected together all the thrown out irons — like iron your clothes — and balanced them until he made a stack of them with his epoxy so they would stand by themselves. His mother shook her head, saying she thought they were nice, wondering what would become of her son who busied himself making stuff out of junk. Senseless, she thought.

A few days after he and Moxie were abandoned. Zane had a thought. They needed to get someone to pay attention to them and the junkyard. They needed to eat. They were running out of food. His father had been paid to be the keeper of junk. Now, well, no one had come to pay. So he had to do something.

First of all, Zane thought, if you grow up with junk, after a while you begin to see the beauty of it. And if you have been abandoned in the junkyard like the junk itself, well then you need to figure out how to use what you have to get attention. Then at the same time, see if you can express your sadness and loneliness in the possible beauty of the junk.

It had been only three days ago that Zane suddenly

jumped up and ran around the junkyard. Moxie ran after him, wondering what this was about. Zane stopped and looked at each of the many small sculptures he had made and realized that he could take his epoxy and make letters. The letters would make words. He could create a tower of letters to make a word to rise up over the junkyard walls. Moxie barked. Zane looked at the huge junk mountain at the center of the yard. "There," he pointed.

Moxie barked Yes!

Zane had built three letters so far. Someone's got to see that, he thought.

Zane cut more letters out of old cardboard, rotted crates, worn and rusted metals and leftover plywood. He would use these to make letters to continue to build his word tower. They lay on the ground looking as lost as Zane felt, but also looking possible. Zane thought about "possible."

One good thing about this madcap busy-ness was that it took your mind off of other, not-so-fun-things.

"Got to keep going," he said.

"Woof" said Moxie, wagging his tail.

Zane began building new letters in earnest, using the beautiful junk to put up his tower. What fun!

An **O** was easy. There was lots of circle stuff around the yard. This one was a rusty something he painted red stripes on. **N** was harder — …he found three lovely spikes and put them together to make a fun "N." Nice.

Zane felt better. He saw right away that he had created **ON** which was the reverse of NO… yet no one came and knocked on the worn Junk Yard gate to offer him a sandwich or Moxie a nice juicy bone.

Another D… well, maybe a good sign: two D's so far   Dancer   and   Dancer.

Maybe this meant hope… Moxie barked, yes!

…and now, another N, only this time a beautiful gold frame. How did this get into our junkyard… hmmmmm. Well, surprises are good, right Moxie!

Moxie waged his tail…

When it came to **A**, Zane realized he liked it instinctively. A seemed good and right, no wonder it was the first letter of the AlphAbet, it was important. This A would have dots on it, 'cause he had cut it out of some metal flooring. I am getting good at this, he thought, and Moxie barked "Yes." But Zane's sadness and loneliness was still with him. He felt like he had imprisoned himself. No one had come to the yard yet. Couldn't they SEE his tower of letters? Though he was willing to admit that no one might know what **"ANDONEDZ"** meant.

No one would know that an A and a B were coming.

Zane was working hard on the "B" and the "A" to finish the top of his word when he and Moxie heard someone at the front gate.

"Hi…" she said.

"Oh, you scared me," Zane said even though he had been hoping someone would come.

"What are you making with those letters?" she said, pointing to the tower.

Zane felt foolish as he held up the last two letters he was finishing.

"Isn't that funny," she said. Moxie and Zane didn't understand what was funny, but they smiled at her. She was a pretty girl, just about Zane's age.

"My name is Abby Banning," she told them.

They looked at her and then she laughed and pointed at the letters. "**A** for Abby and **B** for Banning. See?"

Then they all laughed. Oh yes, oh yes, we see... Moxie barked and jumped up and down. Zane didn't seem to know what to say, so he said, "Why don't you come in?"

"Okay," she said. "I have never been in the junk yard. It looks different... ah, interesting."

"Would you like to have these letters?" Zane held out the A and the B to her.

Abby took the letters and looked at them. Then she looked at the unfinished tower of letters and held them up to the sky and the tower. She spelled it out:

"A B A N D O N E D Z"

Abby turned to Zane, dropping the letters and reached out to give him a hug. "You must be very sad and lonely."

Zane wondered how she knew that, but it felt good to be hugged.

Moxie barked at Abby, who reached down and picked him up. "You're sad too, I'll bet."

Two kids and a dog stood there like statues in the junkyard looking at each other. Zane wondered what to say to this girl. Abby wondered what to say to Zane. Moxie was feeling the best because Abby was holding him.

Finally Zane said, "…would you like some coffee?"

"Yes, I would…" said Abby who carried Moxie into the living hovel where Zane led them to.

"This doesn't look like a very comfortable place," she said.

"Well, it's home," said Zane.

Zane explained that the living hovel had been just like this ever since he could remember. Oh, his father had made small improvements and plugged holes in the walls from time to time. Sometimes, Zane said, when his mother would venture out of the junkyard, she might bring flowers back that she found in some field nearby and decorate the doorway. It was made from the back of a truck, as if the truck had been driven into the hovel. His mom also put flowers near their eating area.

Abby nodded dutifully at Zane's explanation of how his "home" came to be, but inside she felt horrified that someone her age, who seemed to be so bright, should have to live in a place like this. But Abby knew that now was not the time to say anything.

Zane continued to explain how his home had come to be. Abby could see that the eating area was large and had an ornate wooden table in the middle. It had glass imbedded in its surface. Abby ran her hand over the table. It felt oddly smooth. It seemed quite out of place in this makeshift space. She looked around. The walls were soft, covered with old blankets and truck tarps and some colorful rugs. The puzzle was in the middle of this hovel, a whole kitchen, with all the things for cooking, just like in a regular home.

Zane explained that the kitchen had been brought whole and complete to the junkyard to be thrown away. His father, who had been a plumber before the family fell on hard times, had moved all the various parts of the kitchen into the hovel and connected everything up. His father's plumbing skills had came in handy. Zane had tried to learn from him.

Abby touched his arm. "How about that coffee?"

After they settled with their coffee outside the door to the living hovel Abby wasn't sure if she should ask Zane where he went to school, or if he went to school. Abby crossed her fingers. "Where do you go to school?"

"Oh, at Central High, though I don't go all the time. I am, uh, was a junior."

"Oh, me too! I am a junior at a high school out in the 'burbs."

Zane shrugged. He didn't know any other kids or schools. There was a long pause which Moxie took advantage of by coming over to Abby and sitting beside her. He knew she would pet him.

Finally Abby asked, "Why did you say that about school? Don't you go all the time?" Abby paused for a moment and then said, "Where did your folks go?"

Zane shrugged. "Don't know…"

"Think they'll come back?"

"Don't know…" Zane looked at Moxie. "I don't think so."

"Were they good to you?" Abby asked.

Zane sighed. "Oh, I don't know. They weren't very good to each other. My mom was unhappy a lot. My father, well, he's kind of hard to get along with. You know?"

"Yes," she said. "I know."

Zane didn't say anything to that.

No one said anything for a while.

"Well," Abby said finally, "you are spelling A B A N D O N E D up there… so you must feel that way, right?"

She paused. "There is another way to feel

about this… 'cause you didn't seem to have a very joyful family…"

She looked right at Zane. "Maybe you should feel free. Maybe this could be a good thing." Abby smiled and put her coffee cup down. She moved over to sit beside him. "I wish I was free."

Without thinking, Zane blurted out, "What do you mean? Aren't you free?"

"To tell the truth, no… nope. I feel like my head is in a pillow. What would your head be like in a pillow?" She glared at Zane.

"Ah… well, stuffy, I guess. Drowned in feathers?"

Abby tried to smile. "Suffocated."

Zane nodded. He looked at her. She had a soft yellow blouse on over jeans. Her hair was short and fluffy and blond. She had green eyes. He was afraid to say that he thought she was pretty and smart and he was sorry she felt like her head was in a pillow. Abby watched him while he thought about this. "It's okay," she said, "you don't have to say anything. But I have the feeling you understand what I am saying."

Zane nodded. Abby nodded back. "I have to go. Thanks for sharing and showing me around your, ah, interesting place."

They walked outside and she looked up at the letters again. She held out the A and the B to Zane. "Want to put these up now?"

"No, they're for you."

"You going to go to all the trouble to make two more?"

"You think we," Zane pointed to Moxie, "you think we are free?"

Abby nodded.

"What would you do if your head wasn't in a pillow?" Zane asked.

"I would throw away your A N D O N E D and do something else."

"What?" Zane pointed to the tower of letters. "I was hoping to get some attention… maybe get someone to bring us some food. People still come here and leave their junk and I take it. Maybe I can be the new junk guy."

Abby shook her head no.

"What do you mean?" asked Zane.

"Oh, I don't know what I mean – you just don't look like a junk guy. You are doing some interesting things here. Why not do something *really* interesting?"

They looked at each other. Zane shrugged. Moxie wagged his tail. Abby looked around the yard and up at the tower. "Well," she said, "you know what I thought when I first saw those letters you made up there?"

"No…"

"I thought you going to make a scrap metal alphabet tower over the junkyard."

"You thought that even though it wasn't spelling out the alphabet?"

Abby reached out and took Zane's hand. "Listen, I hope you won't ask me a bunch of questions, but I am wondering if you would let me come back here. I could help you make a tower of the alphabet… if you'd let me… you said you were having fun with your A B A N D O N E D tower. An alphabet tower will still get attention, but it will be about something. About something different from being lost and abandoned and lonely and sad…" and Abby began to cry. She leaned over and cried on Zane's shoulder while he wondered what was happening and what to do and… Moxie came over to Abby and whined anxiously.

Abby looked down at Moxie and then up at Zane. "I can't tell you why, I just can't. You'll have to trust me, and there is no reason for you to do that either. All you need to do is promise me is that while I'm here working with you, you won't touch me. Okay. I know that sounds, like, weird, but I guess I need you to promise that to me."

Zane was quiet. Moxie moved over and sat next to him, knowing somehow that things were strange here, that Zane needed him.

Zane and Moxie looked at Abby for a long time. Finally, Zane said, "You need to be careful, don't you?"

Abby nodded.

Zane said, "Some one hurt you, right?"

Abby nodded yes, and then shook her head no.

"You will come back here to help us?"

"Yes, I want to do that."

"Soon?"

"Yes, soon."

"Okay, we'll be here and we won't touch you. Promise."

"Okay. Goodbye…"

That night while Zane was fixing Moxie's dinner dish he said, "She's a pretty nice girl, eh, Mox?" Moxie brushed Zane's leg. "Smart, too… that idea about the alphabet tower is a good one. I hope she comes back."

Moxie brushed Zane's leg again. Zane took that for a yes.

While he was up on the tower taking the letters down Zane was glad he had given A and B to Abby. He liked her new idea. From that height on the tower, Zane could see the town around the junkyard.

"Well," he said to no one, "this place is going to be pretty different now that we have a new, fun idea."

The junkyard seemed to be organized, if such a word could be used about a junkyard, into categories:

There were flat sheets of junk.

There were piles of scraps of metal. These seemed to have new possibilities because they came in many irregular shapes.

The only white objects were the lost appliances. There were For Sale signs on some of them, as if these stoves, washers and dryers had fallen into the wrong place.

There were no cars… but there were piles of old fashioned objects – irons, lanterns, signs – rusty and lost from not only their owners but from time itself.

Everywhere lay scattered boxes of rusty hardware. There was a big pile of old and new tin cans.

Zane said to Moxie, "Quite a place we have here. I think Abby showed us that we have a chance at something new, maybe different. I think we can make something beautiful out of this, and maybe get that attention we wanted."

Abby didn't come that day. Or the next day.

Finally Zane and Moxie looked up at where the alphabet tower would be and were pleased to see that Zane had left the Z there. They smiled. They had to begin somewhere, might as well start with Z.

The next day began with Moxie showing Zane some bent metal. Zane fashioned a Y out of the metal and it was heavy.

They smiled. This is fun. Crazy **Y**.

Zane had fun making this letter **X** out of the colorful odd cans and tin boxes. He still did not realize that the letters would have to be higher to be seen by the outside world on the top of his junk mountain. He felt anxious and wondered when Abby would come back to help him make more letters?

Late that night, when Moxie and Zane were deep in sleep, Zane felt something fall next to him. He woke with a start and reached for the alarm clock so he could hit whoever had fallen onto his bed.

"Zane, Zane… it's me, Abby. Don't, ah, don't do anything – it's me, Abby."

Moxie sniffed her to see if she was telling the truth. He made a snuffly sound. Yes, it was Abby.

"What are you doing here?" said Zane, full of sleep.

"I, ah, I was out walking in the park and then I decided to go over to the river."

"Why?" Zane switched on the light.

She shrugged, "Don't know…" She was dazed.

"I have to get home soon. What time is it?"

Zane looked at the alarm clock in his hand. "Two-thirty. Pretty late for a walk, isn't it? You're crazy to be out alone at night like this."

Abby nodded, "I guess I am crazy… wish that were funny… I wish…" She began to cry.

Zane looked at her closely. "What happened to your face?"

"I fell the other day… ah, down some stairs… does it look bad?"

"No, not too bad, but not too good either."

"S'okay…"

"Is that right? You okay, Abby?"

She shook her head, no. "I just needed some one to look at me to make sure it was me." She looked right at Zane. "Is it me, Zane?"

"What's up with you? Of course it's you. Who would it be? Abby, I need you to tell me what's going on."

"I'll tell you someday, but not tonight... someday, Zane, trust me, please... I got to go now. My mom is still asleep."

Before Abby got up, she gave Zane a hug.

"Thanks... thanks..." and she ran out of the hovel and away.

Zane looked at Moxie. Moxie looked at Zane. They both wondered what had just happened.

The next morning, Zane found an **S** hidden behind a pile of tires.

He continued to pick up junk and look at it carefully as if it could be — he looked at the S — Special. After all, if you think Something is Special, then it can become Special, almost as if you had given it permission.

Moxie watched Zane. He didn't wag his tail. Moxie was a worried dog today after what had happened last night. He was a smart enough dog to know that Zane really wasn't thinking about the junk today.

Zane had the good judgment not to put the S on the tower yet. It would be out of order. He wanted Abby to come back — to help make Moxie and him feel Special.

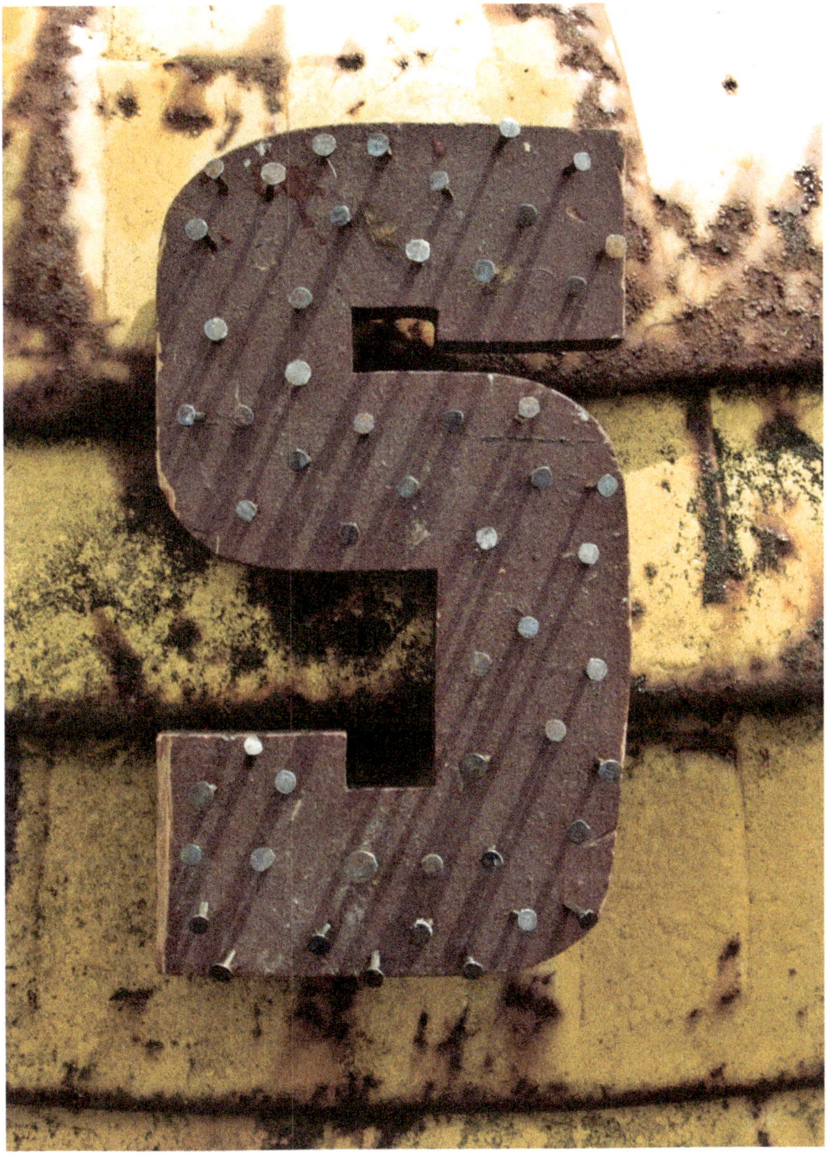

So, **W** was next. W W W   Mmmm, a complicated letter, he thought. But maybe it was simpler than that. Maybe Zane was thinking of W — as in WE, but all he found was a piece of flooring that he could cut up to make W, as in WE or as in WE Three.

Now **V**, he thought. V for what? V for Very Confused...

Zane realized he had never felt this way before... he seemed to miss Abby more than his folks. How could that be? Well, don't be so dense, he thought. Moxie barked, yes. How could he know that, thought Zane?

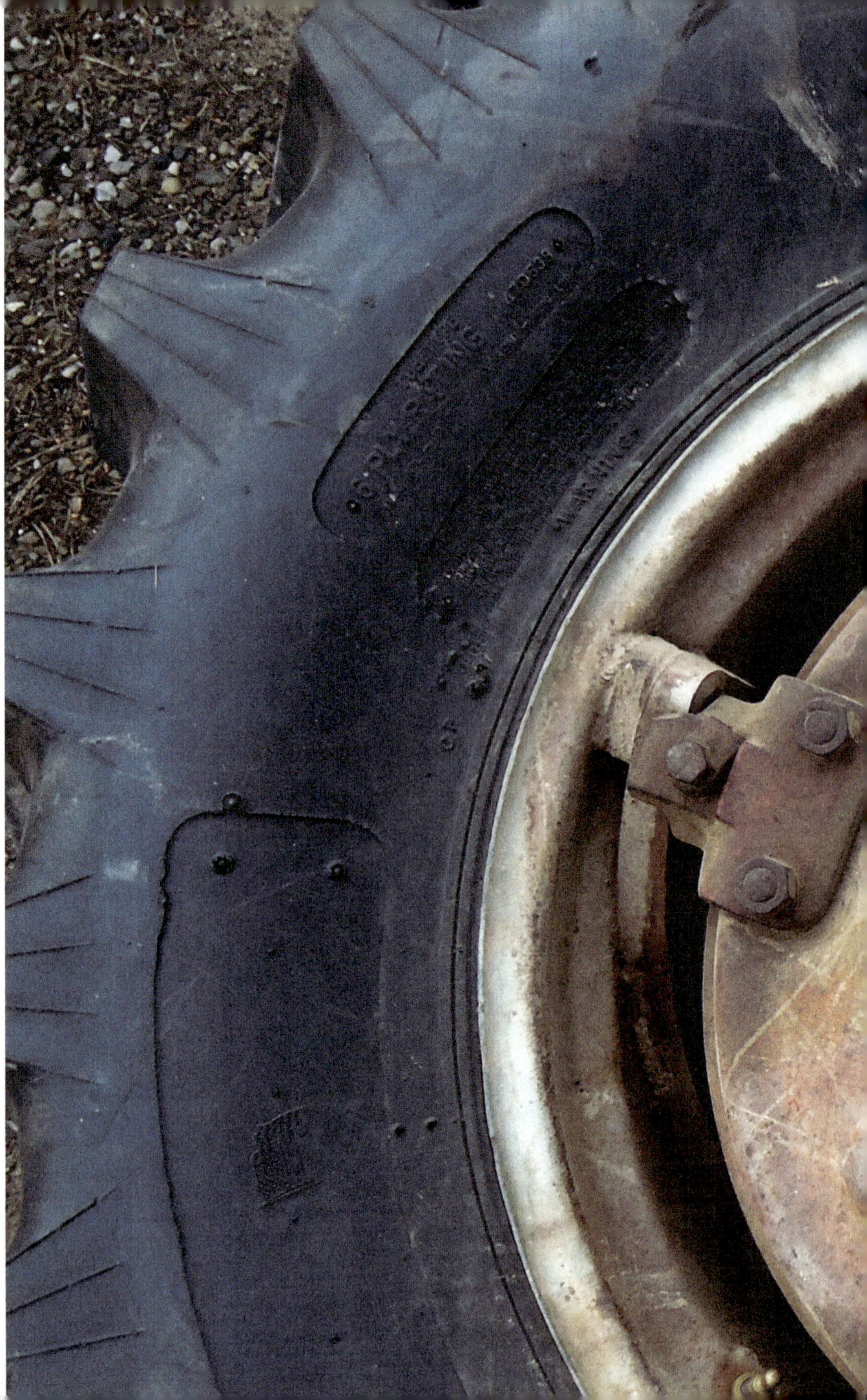

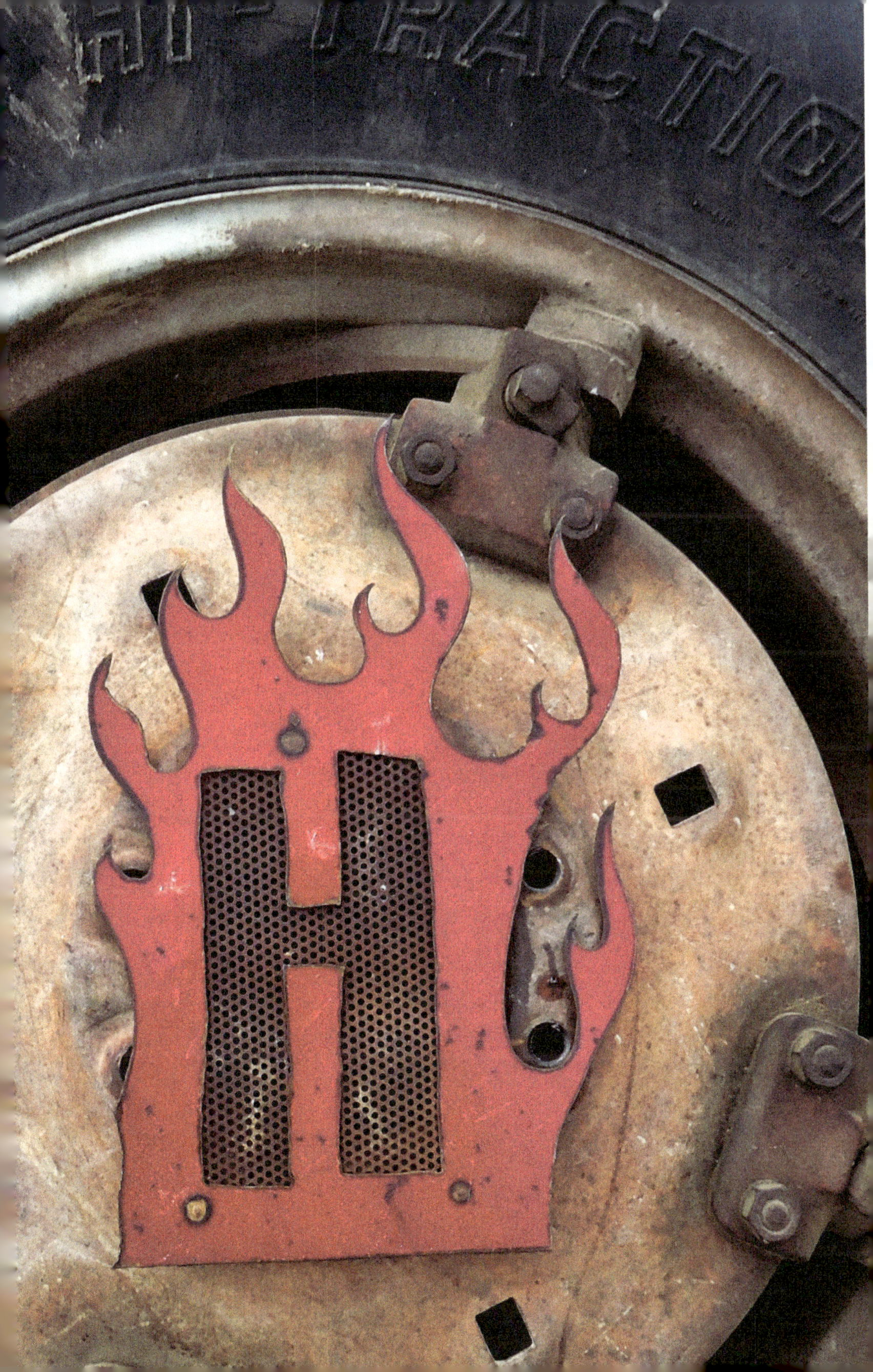
HI-TRACTIO

In the end, Zane wished that **H** came before V so he could put that up next – VH

Very Hopeful.

That night, Zane and Moxie ate the last of the food.

Zane wondered what they would do tomorrow, and the day after tomorrow, until the tower got tall enough to get some attention, which might bring… help.

He sat on the edge of his bed and wondered why he stayed in the junkyard. He could have taken Moxie and left, if there had been a place to go. He could have found his teacher – she was a good person. She might have had an idea.

Then he remembered what Abby had said about A B A N D O N E D and about freedom.

Was Zane free? Sure, he was free. Now he was trying to act free and not abandoned. So did that mean he was free to leave, to find another place for himself and his dog? Why not? It was then he realized that he was waiting for Abby to come back. She had said she would and he believed her.

He must have had some sense then, in the beginning, that he needed to stay here in the junkyard. Yes, his folks might come back, but then again they might not. But in any case, he was here. Only today he had run out of food. He had met Abby, and she would come back. Now she had a better idea with the alphabet tower. He didn't have that before and now he did. Maybe this could turn out all right. How is a person to know, really know? He needed to remember this when he got to R in the alphabet – Really Remember.

The next morning, while Zane and Moxie were still asleep, they heard a noise. This time, more aware, Zane jumped out of bed. He ran to the door in his shorts, and there was Abby, smiling, with two grocery bags full of food.

"Hi," she said.

"Hi," he said, realizing he was not dressed.

"Woof," Moxie said.

"Well, come on, sleepyheads, time to get up, eat and make some letters for our alphabet tower. We can do this!"

Moxie said, "Woof, woof!" Zane nodded, "Woof."

He smiled and stepped aside to let Abby into the hovel. "Yes, we can do this," he said.

After breakfast Abby looked around. She found the junkyard more interesting than she expected, but she needed to see the possibilities in all this stuff. The center of everything was the junk mountain, and she looked up with a smile to see Zane waving at her, putting up a **U**…

Abby wondered at how things work out – on the day she came Zane put up a U which was, in real life, a large horseshoe and what did that signify? Well, dumbhead, Us! Abby smiled at the horseshoe and thought, maybe it could be a special horseshoe and bring us Good Luck. Horseshoes can do that, she hoped. Then Abby asked Zane if he felt better.

"Yes," he said. He admitted that he liked her company and looked forward to her help. That made Abby smile.

"But," Zane added, "there is still a small hole in my heart." Abby noted that Zane did not mention feeling free.

"Do you think you are to blame for your folks leaving?"

He nodded. "Maybe we all wonder if we are good kids."

Abby nodded back. "Sure, but maybe this was not your problem. Maybe it was their problem. You think?"

"Well, I guess everyone has problems." He looked at her, understanding that she might have even bigger problems than he had.

Zane said, "I know that you have problems and they must be big ones." Abby smiled and then made a face at him. They were sitting outside in the late afternoon. Zane looked right at the sunset and said, "Well, I guess it might be true that what happened to my folks, their bad luck and fearfulness – all that has nothing to do with me."

Abby nodded. "So whose problem is it?"

"Right, it's not my problem…"

Abby finished the sentence for him. "So it's their problem and it has nothing to do with you. Now you can be like a bird and fly over their mistakes. You are free to begin to make your own new thing here… and you got it… the alphabet tower will do it. I just know it, Zane."

She reached over and hugged him.

Zane remembered she had said, "No touching," but he liked her hug, and said nothing.

Zane realized after a while that the sun had gone down. He noticed that Abby had not spoken a word for some time.

"You saw inside that large area where we made the coffee and off to the side in the back, there was a bed there?"

Abby nodded. "That's where you sleep."

"What you didn't see was that behind there is another room in the back where my folks slept. I want you to go back there now and throw out the stuff you don't want and make yourself a bed and a place to be. You got no stuff, right?"

Abby nodded.

"Will that be all right for you?"

"Yes," Abby said. "You are very kind." She touched his hand.

Abby walked back to the room Zane had indicated. It was reached through a series of small hallways, turns really, like a funhouse maze. There were pieces of old billboard signs, abandoned doorways, garage doors, iron gates. Last, there was a large curtain Abby moved aside to enter.

The space where Zane's folks had lived took Abby's breath away. It seemed to belong more outside than inside. There were beds, small tables, and dresser drawers – drawers scattered all around the room. Drawers with no dressers to go with them. There were drawers filled with hats and drawers filled with jewelry. Even some drawers filled with garden stuff like iron frogs.

In a corner there was a pile of large drawers filled with headlights from cars, though there were no cars in the junkyard. There were drawers of flashlights and a drawer of lightbulbs. Mmm, she thought, all that lost light.

Then Abby noticed it was odd that such a dark place had so many broken lights. She thought that Zane's folks must have been so happy with the outside of the junkyard that they wanted it to look the same inside. She giggled to herself. She thought about what Zane had said – if there was anything Abby didn't want, to throw it out into the main room. Well, she thought, this is what they lived with and what he thinks is a normal everyday way to live. Abby's first idea had been to find a way to change where and how Zane lived. Now she shook that out of her mind and yelled to him that the room was fine as it was. That she was going to sleep. They had a big day tomorrow.

When Tomorrow came, Abby didn't even wait to get organized. First thing after coffee, she made a **T**.

Zane and Moxie were surprised that she seemed to have sewn the T together. How could she do that?

Zane didn't waste any time climbing up the tower and placing the T.

Now they were Together, Thinking about the Tower.

Abby grabbed Moxie and began dancing around the mountain of junk. This was so much fun! Zane felt lighthearted. That's the word that came to Zane's mind — lighthearted. What a wonderful way to start the day. Zane looked up beyond the T and pretended that he could see all the way up to A B and C.

He couldn't wait to get started on an L... for Lighthearted.

Just as Zane was climbing off the mountain his hand came on the S he had found before. S for Special. He placed that above the T and then yelled at Abby and Moxie. He pointed to the S and then to Abby and Moxie.

"What can he mean?" Abby said to Moxie.

Moxie knew but couldn't say.

Abby, with Moxie following her around, was starting to see the possibilities in all this junkyard stuff. She laid out small piles of objects and things for tomorrow.

Meanwhile, Zane was assembling what he needed for his next letter – S was in its proper place, so R would be next and he would get Abby to work on Q... but that would be tomorrow.

After a dinner of ham and beans from a plastic container and some of the fresh bread Abby had brought, the lighthearted spell disappeared. Abby seemed distant and sad. Zane waited to see what she might say, and when she said nothing he moved over closer to her and spoke softly.

"Hey," he said, "what's up with you?" Zane was careful not to mention how she had danced the morning away sorting stuff for letters and being lighthearted. Instead, he waited for her to say how she felt now.

He got up and poured them coffee. After many minutes, he spoke softly to her.

"What are you thinking, Abby?"

"I worry about my mom. She's all alone now." Abby paused to look into the distance. "I guess that's good and bad together – does that make sense?"

Zane understood that sense, good or bad, was not the issue. He understood that maybe there was something else. He knew he should not ask too many questions, but then he had to somehow reach her.

How to reach her?

He had an idea for the letter **Q** for tomorrow's addition to their tower. He handed her a bunch of bottle caps, then set the bottle of epoxy down between them.

"Hey, you mind helping me glue these to Q for tomorrow?"

Abby began dipping the bottle caps in the glue and placing them on the letter. She could see that this would be a fine letter. She said softly, "My dad used to beat my mom, and then, when I tried to stop him from hurting her, he hit me, too."

Instinctively Zane reached out to her. "That's not good."

Abby shook her head. No. No.

"Is your mom okay now?"

Abby nodded. "Yeah, she's safe now…" and then her face fell. "We're all safe now." Her trembling shook the letter and all the bottle caps fell on the floor.

Zane reached over to Abby and held her tight. She cried quietly in his arms for a long time, then stopped crying but still didn't say anything. Zane picked her up and carried her back to her room. She is light, he thought, as he looked into her teary face, and I care for her so much. He set her down on the bed, brushed her blond hair away from her eyes and pulled up a broken stool. Zane sat quietly watching her fall asleep.

This is not good, he thought. Something is wrong here, something really wrong… but then Abby had said her mom was safe now. Well, if she was safe that must mean that her father was not beating her mom… so didn't that mean things were better? What were the tears about?

How could he find out without asking a lot of questions she didn't want to answer? How could he comfort her? What could he do for her?

Without answers, Zane finally lay down on the floor beside her bed and fell asleep, reminding himself to wake up before her and leave the room so she wouldn't know he had been there beside her all night. He didn't know about Abby, but it comforted him to be close to her.

The letter **R** was easy, someone had thrown an R away. Zane paused for a moment, his thought was that there was always someone thRowing someone away.

Away is a far place.

Turned out the Q they did last night was just right for the tower after he fixed it up, and he placed it on top, wondering if anyone was seeing what they were doing.

There was a knock on the gate. Moxie heard it first and barked. Zane went to see. It was two women and a man. He knew one of the women. It was his teacher, Mrs. Naramore, a person he had not seen in the last few weeks.

"Zane, oh, good, I've been worried about you," Mrs. Naramore exclaimed.

She looked back at the others. "He looks fine, doesn't he?" The other two nodded. The other woman said to Zane, "I am Mrs. Langley, the mayor's wife, and I want you to know how pleased we are with your artwork!" She pointed at the tower.

Artwork? thought Zane, and then he saw Abby had come up to stand beside him. The visitors from outside nodded at Abby.

Mrs. Langley continued. "I have brought the City Art Gallery Director, Mr. Archer, with me to meet you and ask some questions about your Artwork Tower."

Zane nodded, uncertain what to say.

Abby said, "We're glad you are pleased with our alphabet. My name is Abby, and this is Zane and Moxie. We are a team."

Mrs. Langley looked closely at Abby. Mrs. Naramore asked Zane, "Where are your folks?"

"They are on a... a trip..." he said. "They will be back soon." Moxie barked encouragingly.

"Abby Banning," Zane turned to Abby. "She and I have teamed up to make the tower."

Mrs. Naramore said, "But, Zane, we have some important work to do in class." Zane hesitated. Abby took his hand. Zane answered, "Good. If you'll let us get a bit further on the alphabet tower, I can come back. Right now, we are in a…" Abby finished his sentence, "…at very crucial part."

The three adults nodded as if they understood. Moxie went up to the three visitors as if to be petted. "Nice dog," they said.

Zane said, "I'd really like to be allowed to go on with the alphabet tower first. I mean, everything has been fine here at the junkyard, except that we are running out of epoxy."

Mr. Archer, the Art Gallery Director, said, "No problem, Zane. I have some extra exhibit money left over. I can have someone bring down some, ah, supplies for you."

"And maybe some postage stamps," added Abby.

Zane looked at her, and she squeezed his hand. He nodded.

Mr. Archer said, "All right, and I'll probably send our photographer down along with the supplies to take some pictures. That all right with you?"

Moxie barked, Abby nodded, and Zane said, "Sure, why not?" He looked up at the tower. "Lots of letters to go…"

The gallery director said, "Even better, if you don't mind, we'll keep a photo record of what you are doing from now on. This will be valuable later."

Everyone nodded and smiled.

Finally, the visitors left. Abby said, "They are sure nice folks. Didn't get all riled up. That's unusual."

Zane nodded. He wasn't sure about them, but then nothing bad had happened, so that was good.

Abby said, "Well, great, there's more glue coming …let's look around for some more letters." Zane looked at Abby carefully. She looked happy again.

"Right," he said. "What do you need the stamps for?"

"I just wanted to ask for something unusual. We don't really need any stamps, do we? Or do you want to write postcards to your folks?"

Abby wasn't sure if Zane was smiling or not.

"Let's keep going," Zane said. "They are going to take pictures. I wonder what that man meant when he said, 'this will be valuable later'?" Moxie barked, as if he really knew the answer.

The kids laughed.

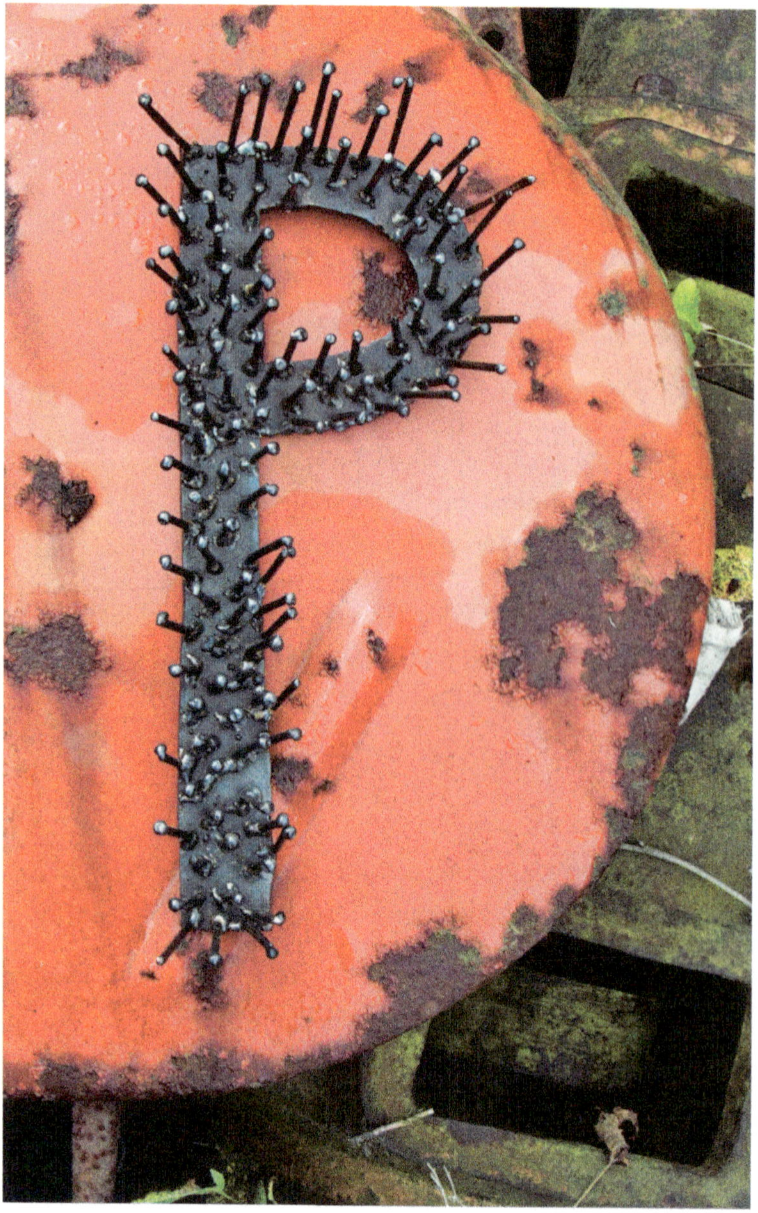

P for puzzled. Right. Zane was feeling puzzled a lot lately.

"So, this is 'artwork'?" said Zane. Seems like there was a lot to be puzzled about.

"Well," Abby said, "those people said so, they must know something we don't."

"You think? What about that 'art gallery guy'?"

"What about him?"

"Did you ever go to the art gallery?" Zane asked, "Sure. My, ah, mother took me a few times… it… was… well, fun I guess… Did you ever go?"

"Nope… didn't even know 'bout it."

The next morning, Abby was not in the living hovel.

Zane picked up the **O** he had made after the group had left yesterday. He went Outside to see that she was sitting Outside the hovel crying. Outside, alone.

"Hey, what's wrong, Abby? You hurt yourself?

"No, I didn't hurt myself, well, maybe I did. I don't know."

"Let me see…" He took her hands.

"No, not there… it's in here." She pointed to her heart.

"What does that..." Zane stopped talking and realized that Abby was thinking about something else.

He sat down next to her and took her hand.

Still crying, Abby shook her head. "You ever seen those news shows on TV about how sometimes, in families, people hurt each other?"

"No, we never had a good TV," Zane gestured behind him to the hovel, "and so I never watched much."

"Well, a father, like they said on these TV shows, he can hurt the mother or sometimes the kids. Did you ever see that?"

"No, I never saw that."

"Well, I saw that and it scared me. You see?"

Zane answered yes even though he did not see. He knew that somehow he had to figure out how to "see" without actually seeing. Abby was seeing something, maybe even right now she was "seeing" something. But what? Zane gently pulled her up. "How about going for a walk, Abby? We could walk over to the park, want to?"

"Yes, I want to... over by the river? Okay?"

As they walked away from the junkyard, Zane looked back at the tower and held up the **O** he had done. With the other hand, he took hers as they walked.

By the time they got to the park, the sun was high in the sky — as if it were looking right down at them. Even though it was a bright day, the park felt mysterious to Zane. He kept looking at Abby, and Abby kept looking at the river and talking to Zane. At one point, she walked over to a bench people could sit on and look at the river.

It was a small river that ran through the town. Once in awhile a flock of geese would settle there. An old woman had come to throw breadcrumbs and cereal for them. Abby watched the woman and the geese. The woman smiled at Abby and the geese honked. Abby liked that. She asked Zane, "What do you think it would look like if we could swim under the river and look up at the feet of the geese?"

"Cool," said Zane.

Abby moved closer to him on the bench. "But what's at the bottom of the river? Things that people throw into the river? Things they couldn't use? Or things they never wanted and needed to get rid of?"

"Sounds like a watery junkyard," Zane said. She should have smiled at his small joke, but Abby looked pretty serious. "Why are you thinking about the bottom of the river?" he said.

Abby was really thinking about the day at school when she got her girlfriend Sally to come up to Bosley, just as he was at his locker, fussing with his stuff. Sally was supposed to bump up against Bosley and say she was sorry, but then give him a big hug. He was a big kid, and not a very nice one either, but Abby said to Sally she wanted to play a trick on him, to take something out of his locker and tease him about it.

Sally was always up for this kind of silliness, so she did it. Right at the exact moment she hugged Bosley, Sally saw Abby reach up and slip a small package out of his locker into her knapsack. Quick, as if Abby did stuff like that all the time.

Just thinking about it, Abby began to breathe more heavily. Zane noticed that and put his arm around her. "You're okay here. You must have been thinking about climbing the junkyard mountain." Abby shook herself. She turned to Zane and gave him a weak smile. "Sure, just thinking of something that happened in school. You know, sometimes it's no fun."

Zane nodded as if he understood.

Zane was getting used to feeling a certain pattern in their lives. He was uncertain about what the pattern might mean, but he "saw" it. He wondered if he was getting better at "seeing." The life he and Abby were leading in the junkyard felt like a see-saw that kids played on, up and down, down and up. But this didn't feel like playing. He and Abby were living a sort of play-pretend game. Things went along well, and then they fell off the edge of the world and things were bad, but they got past it.

See-saw up, see-saw down, an odd game.

Abby made this great **M**…

Zane asked what it Meant.

Abby said Momentum.

Meaning what? he said.

Moving, Moving along… she didn't dare to say to Zane that it was Wrenches, upside down. Ha-ha…

Finally, it was time for **L**. L for lighthearted.

Zane rooted around the yard and found this sort-of L.

Abby Laughed in a Lighthearted way and said it was an L on a sideways X.

Zane felt this was actually like watching a see-saw, moment by moment, day by day, up and down, then there was a knock at the junkyard door. It was the art gallery photographer with the Mayor's wife.

"Hi, kids, we'd like to take some pictures," she said.

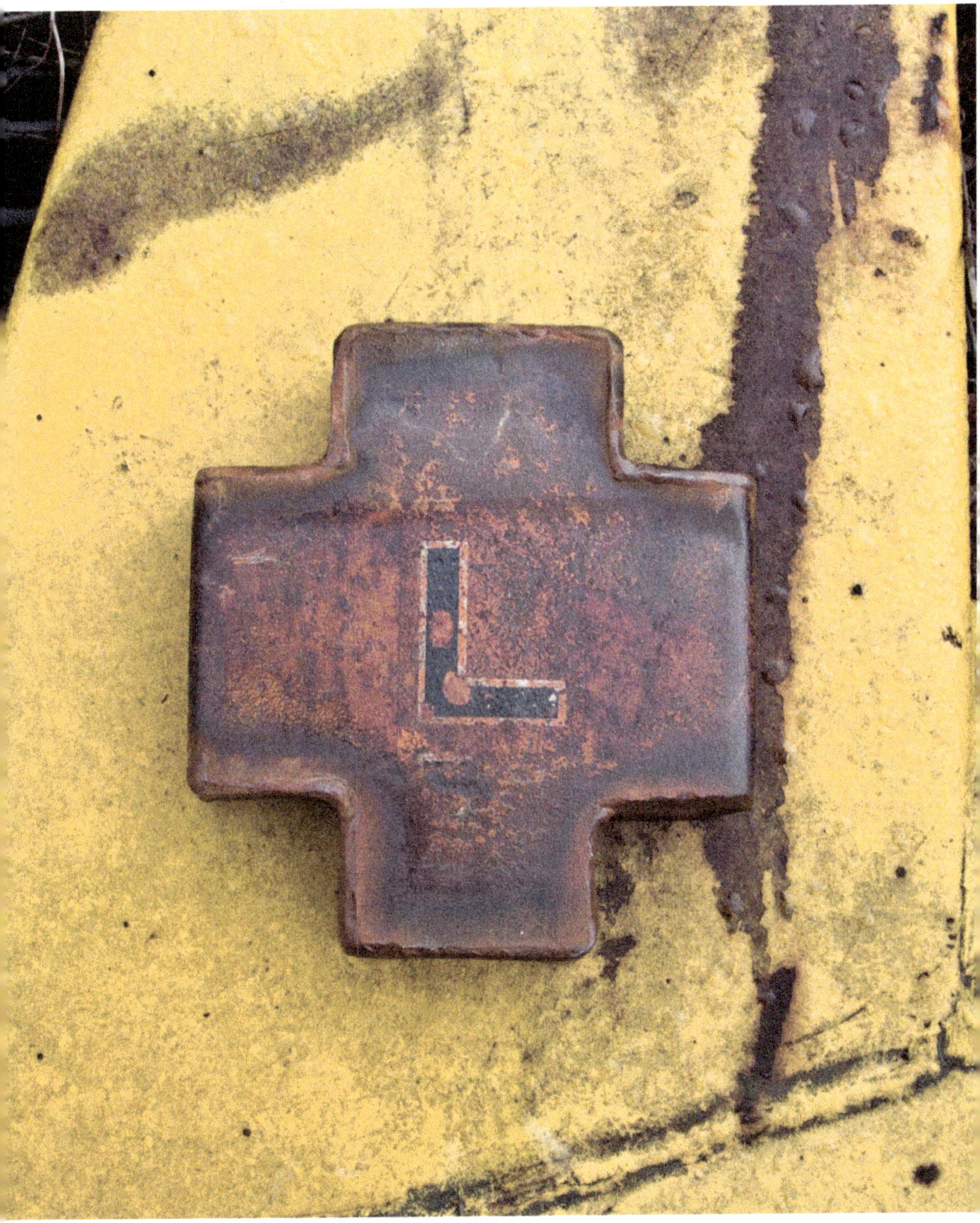
L

When they came, Abby was working on **K**.

She had found a bunch of springs and glued them on the back of the K. That made it jiggle, and it made Abby giggle.

Zane loved it when Abby was happy, so he asked her what the K meant.

"I don't Know, but I feel a lot like this jiggling K…"

The clouds came when the Mayor's wife said to Abby, "Aren't you Abby Banning, the daughter of the policeman who was killed in the Park a while ago?"

Abby held the giggling K to her breast, her face went pale and she nodded.

Yes, she was the daughter of the police officer who was killed in the park. Mrs. Langley touched Abby's arm and said, "I'm sorry, my dear. How is your mother doing? She must be very sad."

Abby nodded and backed away slowly.

Please give your mother my sentiments, we are so sorry."

Zane came over to Abby and whispered something in her ear.

Zane looked at them and said, "Can you give us a moment?"

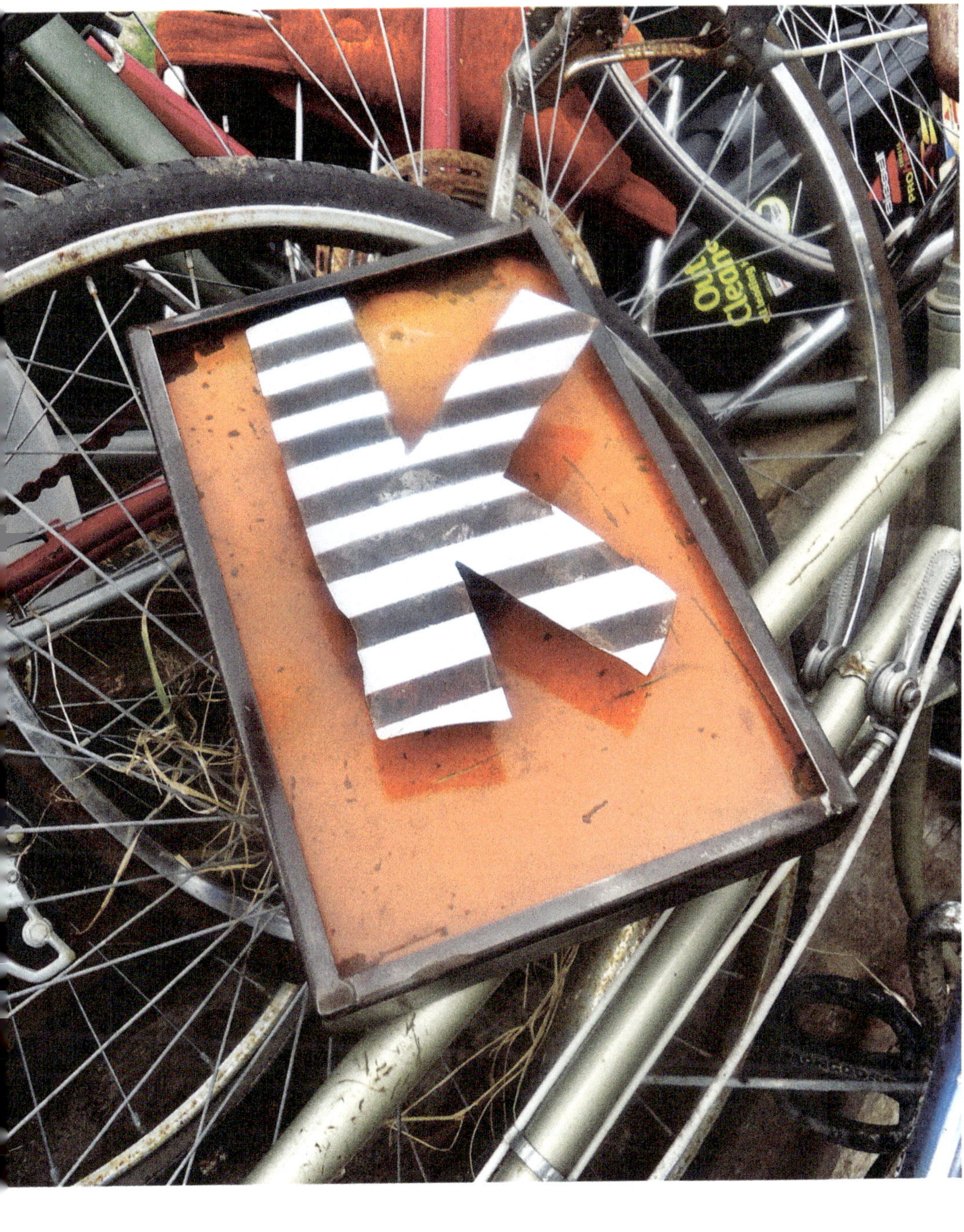

He led Abby over to the hovel and whispered more to her while Abby clutched the jiggling K to her breast.

The photographer was busy taking pictures of the tower. He made quite a production of it.

Then the photographer went over to Zane and asked if he could take pictures of him and Abby.

Abby shook her head, no. Zane went right away with the photographer to take pictures of him standing on top of the mountain with the letters.

When Zane came down, he motioned for Abby to come over to stand for some pictures with him.

Zane put his arm around Abby and whispered that she should smile now. Abby smiled.

The photographer showed them the picture. They seemed happy, but Zane looked at the Mayor's wife and knew something was not happy, but he didn't know what to do or to ask or to say.

Zane was stumped.

Abby whispered in his ear that it was Okay, "I'll tell you later."

Mrs. Langley followed the photographer and Zane and Abby all over the junk yard as he took pictures.

Moxie followed them, too, but he didn't bark.

Abby asked the photographer what he was going to do with the pictures?

The photographer smiled at her, "Use them in the Exhibit." Zane and Abby said it together... "The Exhibit. What exhibit?"

Mrs. Langley spoke up, "An exhibit of your artwork," she said, pointing to the tower. Zane thought, that word again, and looked up at the tower.

The photographer said, "I think the Director, Mr. Archer, is planning to make a show out of your Alphabet Tower."

A show, thought Zane. Abby wondered what Zane was thinking. She snuffled a giggle and pulled him over to their work table. She pointed to it for the photographer and posed herself and Zane at the table, as if they were making letters.

"Hey, this has been great," said the photographer.

Mrs. Langley smiled at Zane. She leveled a look at Abby.

"Please be certain, my dear, to give my regrets to your mother."

Zane looked at Abby with a puzzled face.

Abby forced a smile for Mrs. Langley.

The photographer and the mayor's wife left the **J**unk yard.

Zane felt that using all the metal nuts he needed to make this letter was a symbol of what was happening to him and Abby, the junk yard and the time with Mrs. Langley and the photographer. Like a bunch of metal nuts without any of the bolts.

Zane was feeling torn as well and just a little bit angry. He knew Abby had not been straight with him, yet at the same time, he didn't want to ask her a lot of unwanted questions.

She seemed lost sometimes. She cried sometimes for no apparent reason. She looked off into space a lot, or just up at the tower… or at Zane, as if she wanted to say something to him.

Doesn't she know, Zane thought, that she can say anything to me?

Anything. No, he realized. She doesn't know.

Now that Mrs. Langley had let him know that Abby's father was recently dead he wanted to understand.

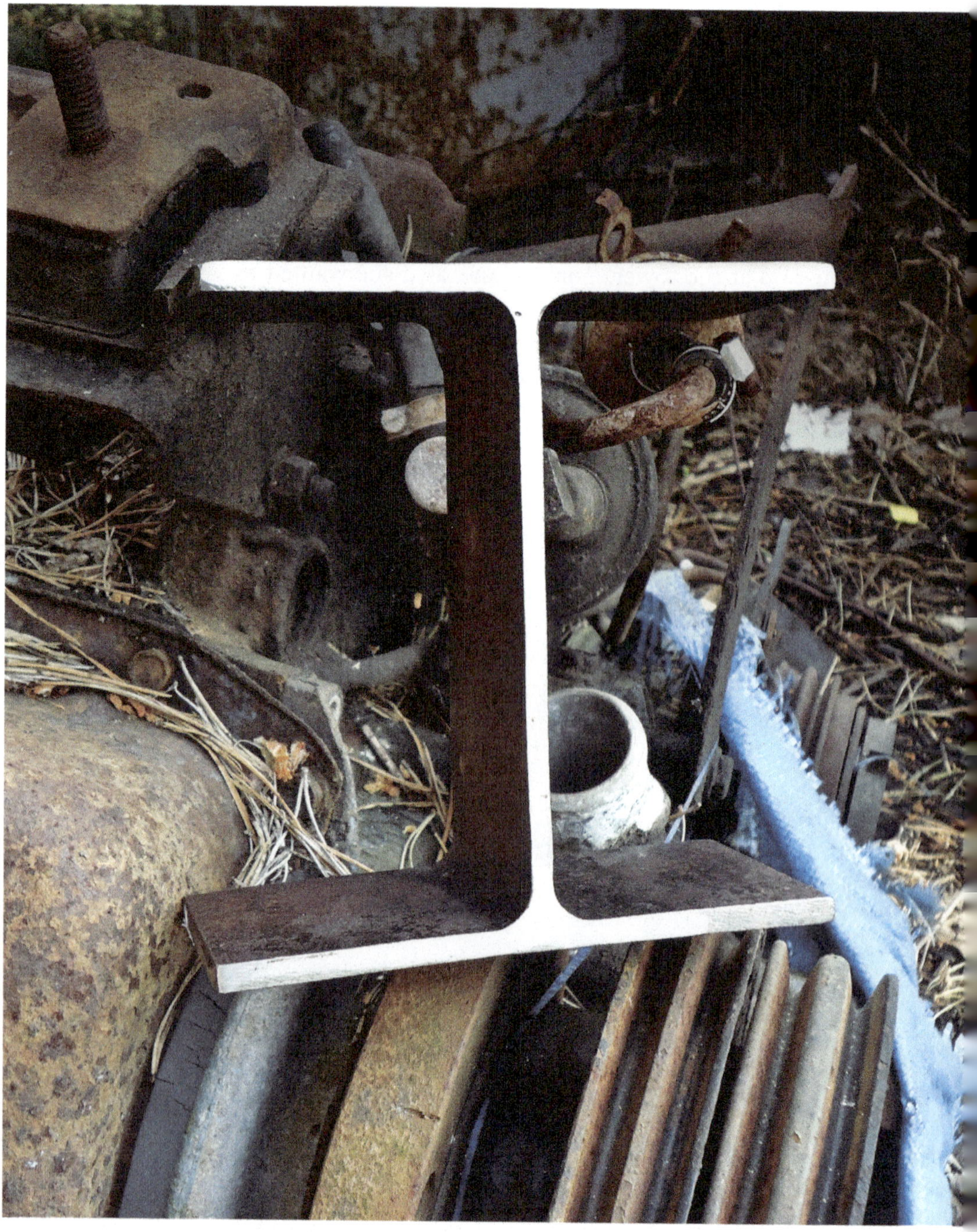

He wanted to try to help. He wanted Abby to know that she could tell him anything, and she would be safe and protected.

Abby was working on **I** when Zane came up to her.

"Don't you think it was time that we talked? I feel like I need some Information."

Abby nodded.

Zane said to Abby, "You know you could say anything to me, anything at all, and I wouldn't think less of you or get mad at you or not like you any more. I think you are very special, Abby. Do you know that?"

Abby smiled. Smiled big, and then started crying. Zane sat her down on the soft bench and put his arm about her. They stayed that way for a long time… until Zane asked, "Why didn't you tell me about your father?" Then Abby started talking in a trembling voice.

"You are such a sweet person, and you have been so good and patient with me – I have never had this…"

Abby cried some more.

Finally, she stopped crying and looked at Zane. "Do you remember when I told you what I saw on the TV about the family where the father beat the mother and then sometimes the child? What I didn't say was that he often threatened that he would kill them. Then one day he killed the mother and then killed himself. The father did all that even though he told the mother he loved her."

"How could anyone do that, Zane? How could you say you love someone and then hurt them? But that's what my father did to my mother – and if I tried to protect her, which happened more and more, then he would hit me, too, but that would be after he said I was a good kid and he loved me. He told my mother he loved her, I heard him say that. But then another time he would hurt her and say bad things to her. One time he broke her arm, and as I was trying to stop him, he almost broke mine, too. It took a long time for my mom's arm to heal, but she said it was all right – she said that to me, 'Abby, it's all right.'"

Zane wanted to ask about her father and how he had died. Abby had told him he was a police officer, so he must have died in a hassle with some bad guys, right? What did they call it? In the line of duty? But Zane knew he should keep listening, keep listening. Keep holding on to Abby to be sure... sure of what?

"What I saw was that we were caught in a box." Abby held up a letter she had been working on. It was a letter that was in a box. "This was me and my Mom — **G** for Good people caught in a box... and even though we were being beaten and hurt, it was supposed to be all right until I saw the TV show and knew that my mom could get killed. I love my mom and I didn't want her to be killed like that mom on TV. The father on the TV, he killed himself after he beat the mom to death. Abby paused and then said, under her breath, "… **G** for gun."

Zane froze as he heard Abby tell this story. He still had his arm about her, but he noticed that at some parts in her story, he tightened his arm so much that it must have hurt Abby… but she didn't say anything. They sat there for a long time thinking about Abby's mom and the family on the TV news.

Zane thought, how can I have this frozen feeling when I feel like I am caught in a hell with Abby?

Zane lifted Abby up until they were both standing, but still hugging. He whispered in her ear, "We have to move on here, Abby. We can't let this make us into junk" – he gestured around him – "so let's do something to take our minds off this. How about a walk along the river? Or we could go out and get some ice cream and think about what that photographer guy meant when he said the pictures will be useful later..."

Abby put her finger on his lips and said, "You are sweet, and you are right – we need to find a way to put this behind us. How about we create a new letter of the alphabet to help us move on?" Her eyes twinkled, and Zane knew that they had put the dragons behind them, at least until the next time.

"Great," he said.

"Woof, woof," said Moxie.

Abby smiled and kissed Zane on the cheek. She picked Moxie up and, carrying him off, said, "Moxie and I are going to look for a dog-letter-word." Zane stood watching her carry his dog off, Moxie licking her face, and wondered how... Now, what? he thought. Well, she's got a good idea. A new letter of the alphabet... Zane walked back into the hovel to get a snack and think.

Time went by. Zane heard Moxie bark. He heard Abby lifting and throwing junk. Crash, crash... tinkle, tinkle... oh, the joy of junk.

Zane found some things in the house that had spurred his imagination and made him think. He found his mother's hair combs. She loved to put her hair up with these combs, and when she did it was special. It had made his father smile, too. There were some odds and ends, trinkets, sewing stuff – mainly thimbles. Zane wondered why people used thimbles. Then he found a bunch of old mirrors, small ones, and his father's brush, one that he had salvaged from a load of stuff from an abandoned house. It was a fancy brush with a metal back that was all engraved. There were small arrows engraved into the metal and they chased each other in a circle. He took all this over to his work table and began fiddling.

Finally, Abby and Moxie returned. They had found a box of dog collars. Abby said she had tried to get Moxie to wear one, but he ran off. Abby said that Moxie "was his own dog…" Zane agreed. Absolutely. He leaned over and petted Moxie, a dog who was a free spirit. Abby said that they decided their new letter for the alphabet would be this: she held up three dog collars that had been wired together to form intertwining **O**s.

They all laughed and woofed and joined hands and paws and danced around together to celebrate the new letter. Abby said it was a letter-symbol to mean Them, the three of Them together. When she said that, Zane stopped laughing and dancing. He moved off and sat by himself on a rusty tank.

"Uh, oh," said Abby. Moxie whined softly. Abby sat on one side of Zane and Moxie on the other and didn't even beg to be petted.

Abby said, "You know, you have been very caring and kind to me about my… ah, troubles, but you have been hurt, too, and no one takes time to try to comfort you." She held the new letter out to Zane. "This is meant to mean Us – capital U, small s. We are this together… but I am guessing that you wanted to feel that with your own folks, and somehow, well, I guess that seems gone. Maybe not forever, but…" Zane began to cry, and Abby turned and held him tight. Moxie crawled into their laps. He licked Zane's face, and curled up with them. The three of them made quite the family picture. Zane felt it and whispered something in Abby's ear. Moxie heard him and licked his face some more. They stayed that way for a long time while Abby kept whispering in Zane's ear.

"I don't know how I know this, but your folks loved you. They were sad people who didn't know how to show it. You think of them, right? You think of the good moments you had as a family, right?" Zane nodded. "But now, in this moment, you are thinking they are never coming back and you are lost?" Zane nodded again.

"But you just said they didn't know how to love you or each other – and that there were good times when you were a family together. And you remember that."

Abby picked up their new joined letter and showed it to Zane again. "Get it?" she said. Zane lifted his eyes to meet hers. He still looked lost. "The new letter shows you that those good times are still in your heart and that you were together once – and maybe, just maybe – some time way ahead, that might happen once again."

Zane looked like he was beginning to get it.

"And you remember those times when they did love you. Right?" Zane nodded again. "So you have moved from three very screwed up separate circles to this one joined together." She held up the new letter again and wiggled herself and Moxie. "Can you feel us now? Don't we feel and look like this new letter?" Zane nodded and hugged her closely.

"Thank you," he whispered. "Thank you."

Moxie said, "Woof. Woof. Woof."

The next day they argued, yelling and jumping up and down about whether Zane should put the new letter on the alphabet tower. Abby voted YES.

Zane voted NO.

Moxie just sat and acted like he was laughing at them. Finally, Abby nailed the new letter to the front gate and danced around while Zane laughed and clapped. Moxie danced with Abby.

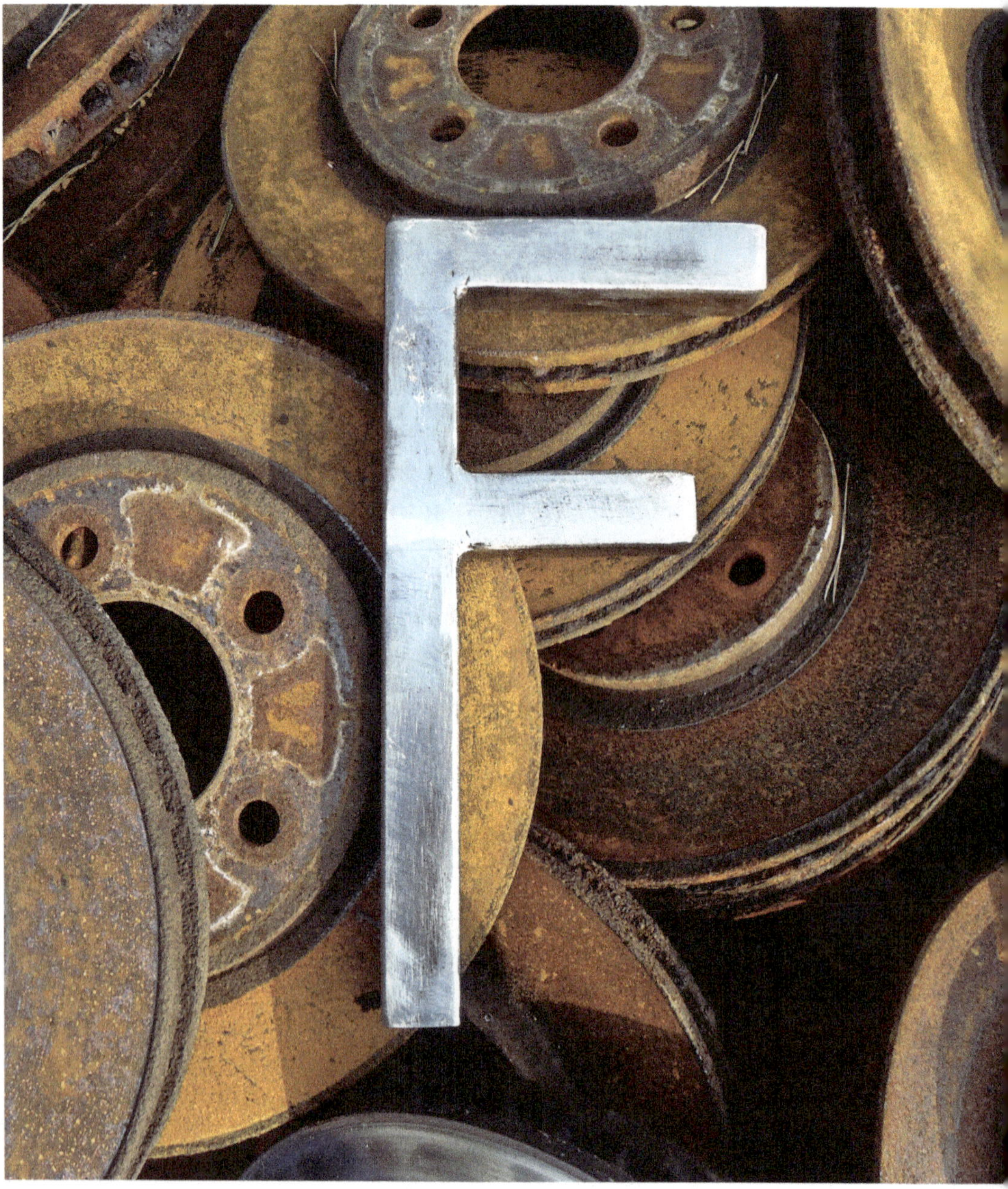

Then, Abby and Zane worked together on **F**.

They both felt like they were close to Fun, Finally Free.

Well, close but not there yet.

One of the regular people who dropped off junk and occasionally actually bought some stuff with money, dropped off some junk and also left the newspaper. On the front page was the memorial for Abby's father. There were pictures of all the officers and a picture of her father.

There was a speech by the mayor. They knew it was the mayor because his wife, Mrs. Langley, was right there beside him – the woman who had come to the junkyard.

Finally, there was a picture of a medal her father was going to receive posthumously.

Zane saw the memorial and tried to throw the newspaper away before Abby saw it. But she took the paper from him and looked at the pictures. There was one of her mom. Abby hadn't seen her mom for many, many days.

Abby dropped the paper on the floor and looked at Zane with her eyes as red as… well, something horrible.

"Zane, I don't care about myself. I killed my father to save my mom. I was afraid that what happened to that family on TV would happen to us – who knows how many people do that stuff. I knew a kid at school who had a gun in his locker and I stole it. I knew my father's beat included a sweep through the park late every night. I went out lots of nights to watch him, nights after he had hurt my mom… I watched him and his every step.

"I tried to figure out how he could be such a good policeman and still hurt my mom. I worried about what might happen… After I stole the gun, I went out one night and waited for him. I watched him come down the path in his dark uniform. I watched him for the last time, and knew that in a moment he would never beat my mom again. She would be safe from him. She would be sad but I would be a better daughter and know that I had saved her life… Maybe that's what my life is for – to save her life and make it the kind of life a good mother should have."

"I stepped into the path in front of my father and looked right at him. He was so surprised. That was the look he had when I pulled the trigger and watched him fall on the grass. He was surprised… that I was there… that I had a gun… that I would pull the trigger and that he would fall down. Before, it was never him who fell down, it was always my mom. It was never him until that night. I walked over to him, knelt down beside him, and told him I loved him. He heard me. I kissed him and waited for him to stop breathing. Then I left. I ran as fast as I could, way over to the river along a path where no one would see me. I threw the gun into the river and I started to run home. It was the middle of the night. My mom was asleep, everyone was asleep, even my father who was on duty was asleep, as he always would be."

Zane interrupted. "That's when you came to me at the junkyard. Right after that. Oh, my, Abby. You killed him – I saw you then. But I never thought you could…"

"I needed to see you, to know that there was some one. You know, a person who you can trust no matter what. So, after being with you, I went home and let myself in.

I went to my mom's room and looked at her. She was safe now. He would never beat her again or hurt her and then say he loved her. I felt good in that moment.

I felt like I had saved her and that was why I was born. Now we could get over having a father and husband who said he loved us and beat us anyway. He was gone and we would forget… it might take time, but we would forget."

Zane and Abby looked at each other for a long time. Abby wanted to ask Zane a question, but she was afraid. Zane wanted to ask her a question, but he was afraid too. Finally Abby said, "Do you hate me now?"

There was a long pause before Zane put his hand on hers. "No, I don't hate you. I see what a – you called it a box – you were in. Both you and your mom. So you saved her life. You did what you thought was the right thing. But how… what about you… Abby, do you think you will be all right?"

"Yes, I will." Abby paused. "You didn't answer my question."

"Ah, yes, well, maybe not. I guess I think you are the bravest person I know to do what you did. You have told me everything and I think you are incredibly brave. No, I don't hate you, I just wish… well, you must have wished for a lot, too."

Abby forced herself to make a small smile. "Well, that's it, Zane. Fearful, Fire, Forget… the real definition for our F – what happens next, Zane?" He pulled her to him and gave her a hug - a big one. F for Friends.

Well, Zane thought, in alphabet terms, it would be E, but somehow no word that started with E felt right to Zane. He longed for – in his innermost feelings – for A B C, new beginnings, a new chance for Abby… and for himself, too.

They sat together on the soft bench for a long time. Zane didn't move his arm from around her. Abby didn't move away from Zane. Moxie jumped onto her lap and licked the tears off her face. None of them realized that they were a family together now. A good family, a safe one, even though they were living in the junkyard. Well, one thing mattered. Zane realized what it was. He said, "Abby, no matter what, I will always be your Friend. I am sorry you had to do what you did. I think you saved your mother, and I am really, really glad you saved yourself to come here and be with me – to build the alphabet tower together."

Zane fiddled with her fingers and then said, "Only one question, Abby."

She looked at him. "Okay... what?"

"Why did you come back here after things were all right at home?"

Zane felt her tremble. "Sure, I guess that's a good question. Things were all right at home, but not with me. I felt I could work out my own stuff better with you here than at home." She looked right at Zane. " ...and I was right."

The next day, they needed something easy, so they did **E** and it was... easy.

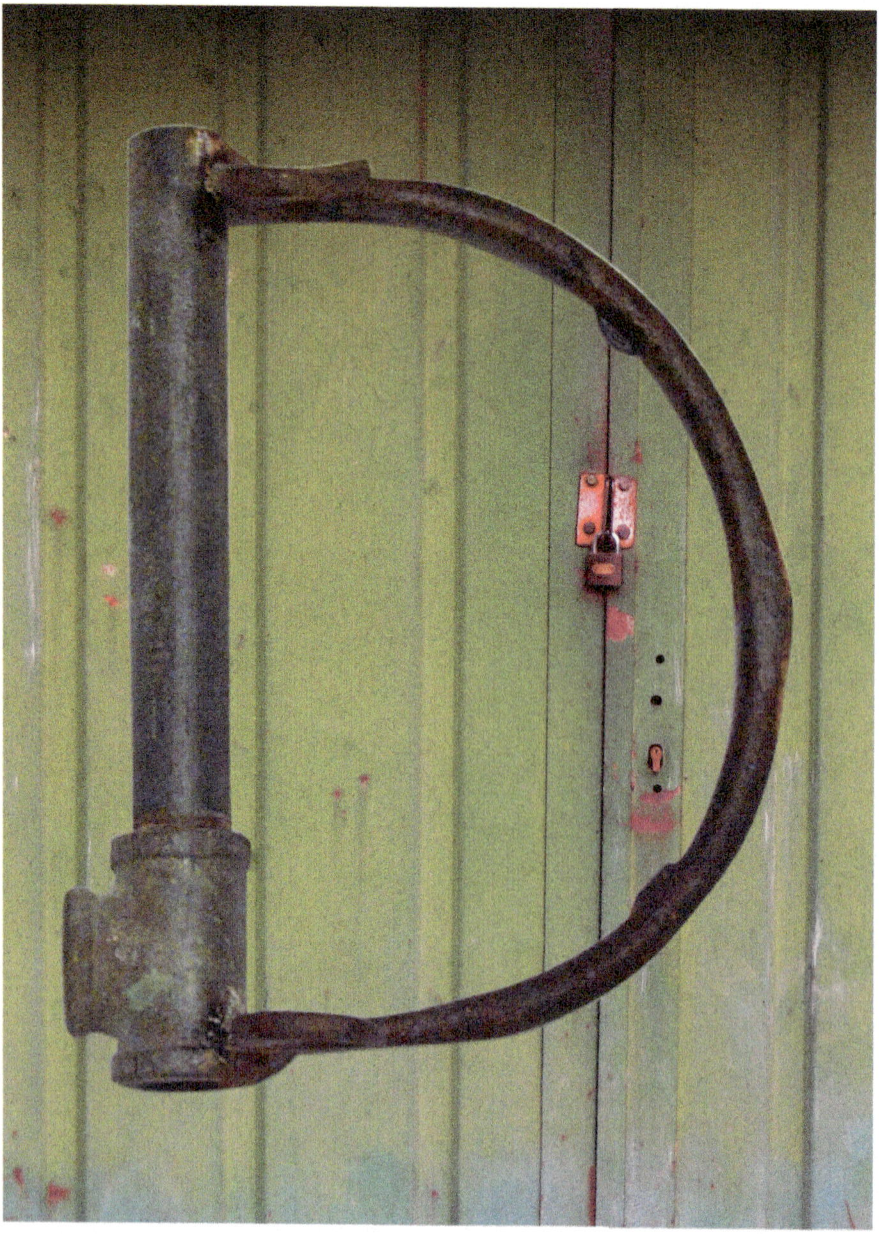

D, on the other hand, was a challenge for all of them.

When Zane climbed up to put D on the tower, he almost slipped and fell. Moxie and Abby were scared. But Zane climbed down and said D was for almost Done.

Abby gave him a smile and a hug.

Now they had only three letters to go and then their Alphabet Tower would be done. D for Done. Done, finally.

What… what… would they do then?

They had seen the pictures in the newspaper of the tower in progress. They knew that the final pictures would be amazing to see, even for them. They were happy, too, because it seemed, the newspaper said, that the Tower would be a good attraction for their town and for the junk yard. Zane wondered what his folks would say when they came back — Abby reminded him that he should be saying "…if they came back…" Abby had tried to get the idea across to Zane that they might never, you know, come back. Moxie was smart and said nothing but mooched to be petted.

First thing the next morning, Zane woke Abby up to show her the A and the B and the C.

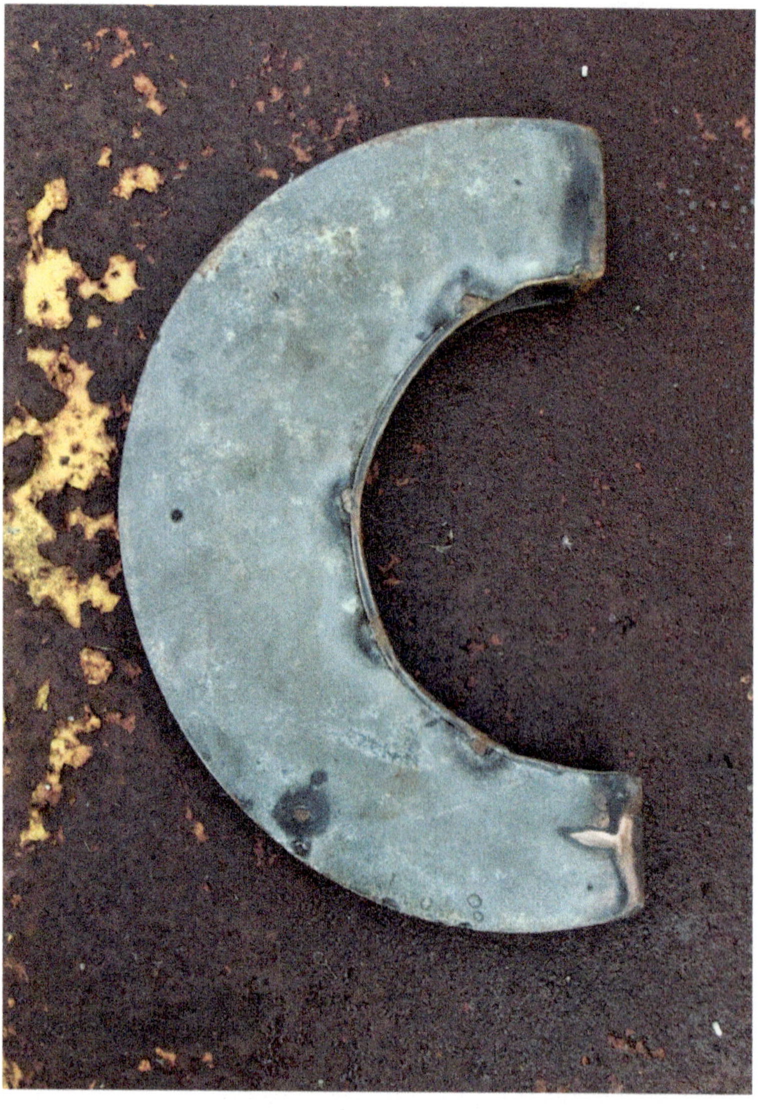

He held up the **C**.

"See this, Abby, this is going to be the letter that holds YOU up — the A for Abby and the B for Banning... the original letters from when we had our heads screwed on backward... from the time we thought we were lost to the time now when we found ourselves. We are going to put these letters up today and say,

"Hooray for us. We built our tower."

Suddenly they heard a lot of noise, like a crowd of cheering people. What could that be? Somebody was pounding on the front gates to the junkyard. As they opened the big gates, it felt as if the whole town was crowding through to see the marvelous alphabet tower. There was that same photographer and then others, too. There were TV news cameras. Everyone wanted to talk to Zane and Abby. Moxie barked happily.

Everyone called them the Alphabet Team. Abby was glad that people understood they were a team. Zane was glad they didn't call Moxie an Alpha Dog. They stayed together as everyone asked questions and more questions. The main question they asked was...

What are you going to do next?

Next??? thought Zane.

They called Zane and Abby visionaries. Moxie barked while Zane wondered... exactly what is a visionary?

Zane realized this was not the moment to try to understand "visionary" or to talk about things like that. Just as he was thinking that, a man walked up with Mrs. Langley. First she gave Zane a hug and whispered in his ear. Then she turned and hugged Abby too, and whispered in her ear. Finally, she introduced the man. "Zane, Abby, I want you to meet my husband, the mayor." Wow, they thought, a real mayor.

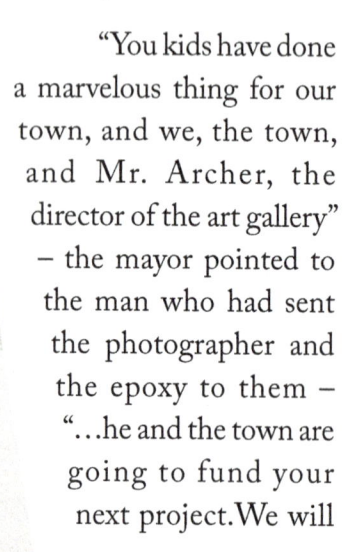

"You kids have done a marvelous thing for our town, and we, the town, and Mr. Archer, the director of the art gallery" – the mayor pointed to the man who had sent the photographer and the epoxy to them – "…he and the town are going to fund your next project. We will supply you with all you need in terms of living expenses and supplies and assistance to do your next project."

Abby and Zane were dumbfounded. The town might think of them like that, but they were just kids living in the town junkyard... but no one said that. It was as if, suddenly, they were the art gallery, or the town square, or visionaries... not just junkyard kids.

Cameras flashed all around them, and all they could see were faces, seemingly hundreds of faces. Then one single face pushed through the crowd. Zane wondered who was this woman was who walked right up to him and gave him a big hug and smile, and then turned right away to Abby and gave her a big smile and hug.

"You kids," she said. "You kids are something." She said it loudly, and everyone cheered.

Then the woman whispered something in Abby's ear, kissed Zane on the cheek, and then disappeared into the crowd as suddenly as she had appeared.

Zane turned a bewildered look to Abby. She smiled at him and squeezed his hand.

The mayor stepped forward again and announced that he had heard Zane and Abby were going to be moving out of the junkyard, and that he would assign new people to care for it…

…but for as long as there was a junkyard, these letters – and he held them up – A gold **Z** and a gold **A**.

…would forever be on the doors to the Yard in honor of the service that Abby and Zane… A to Z have given the town. There was a huge cheer from the crowd. Abby and Zane were heroes, hooray!

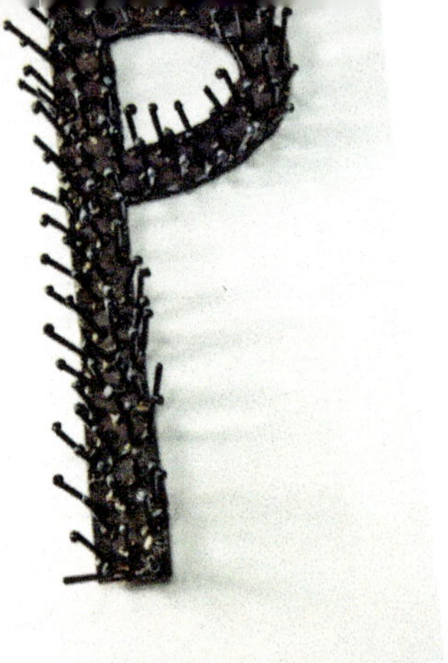
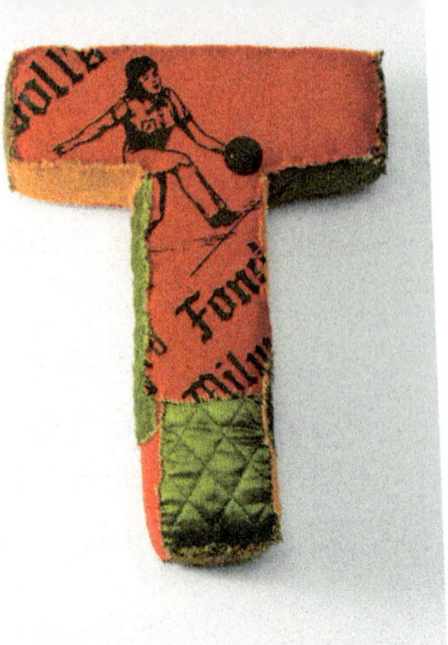
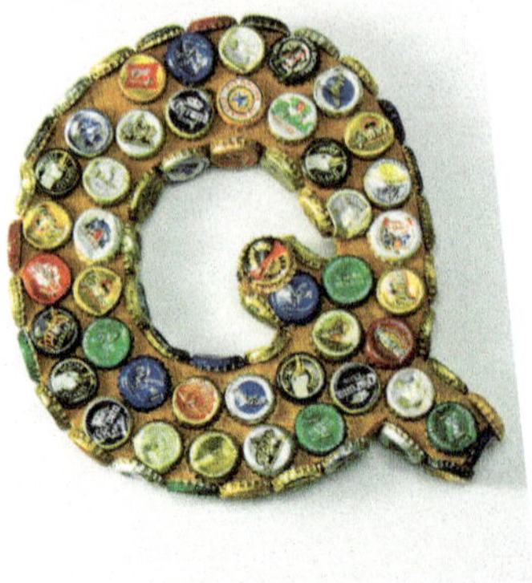
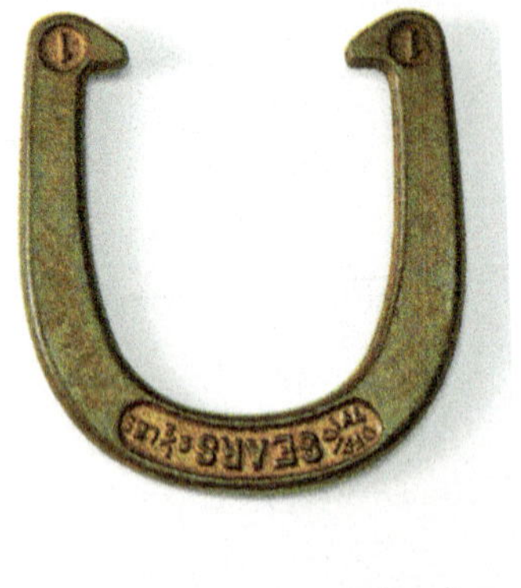
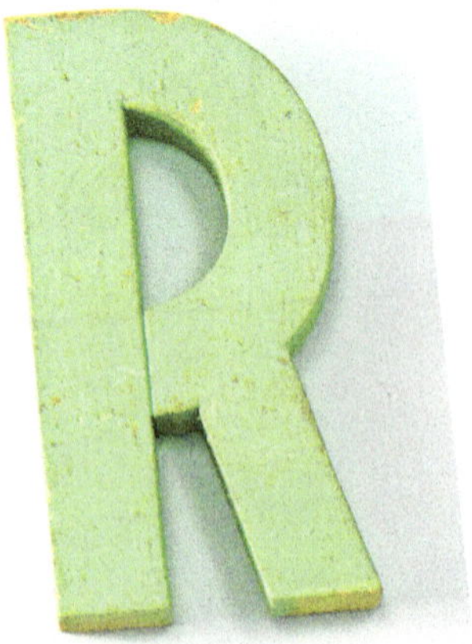
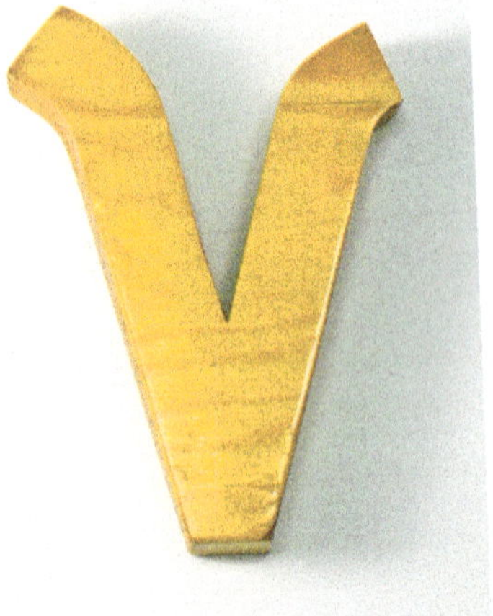
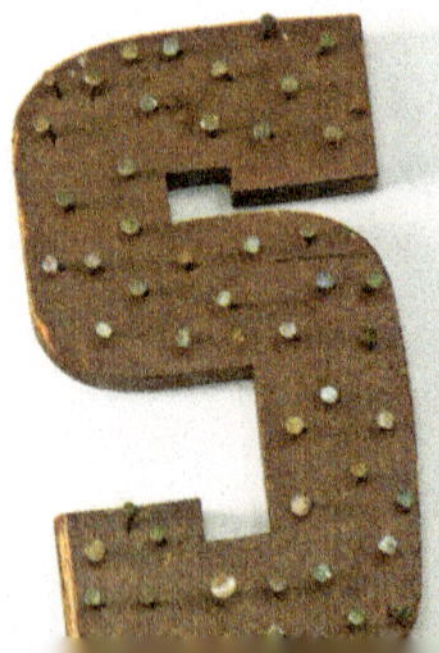
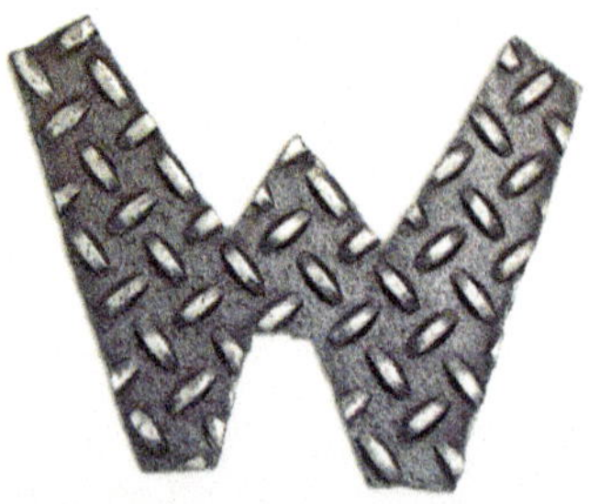

When everyone left and they were finally alone, Abby sat Zane down on the soft sofa and told him that they were indeed moving out of the junkyard. That her Mom had said she wanted both Abby and Zane to come home now. That they could live there with her, for as long as they wished.

Fortunately, Abby's home was located in just the right place to be able to see the Alphabet Tower from the backyard. The Tower would always be there to remind Zane and Abby how to take **Junk** and turn it into **Gold**.

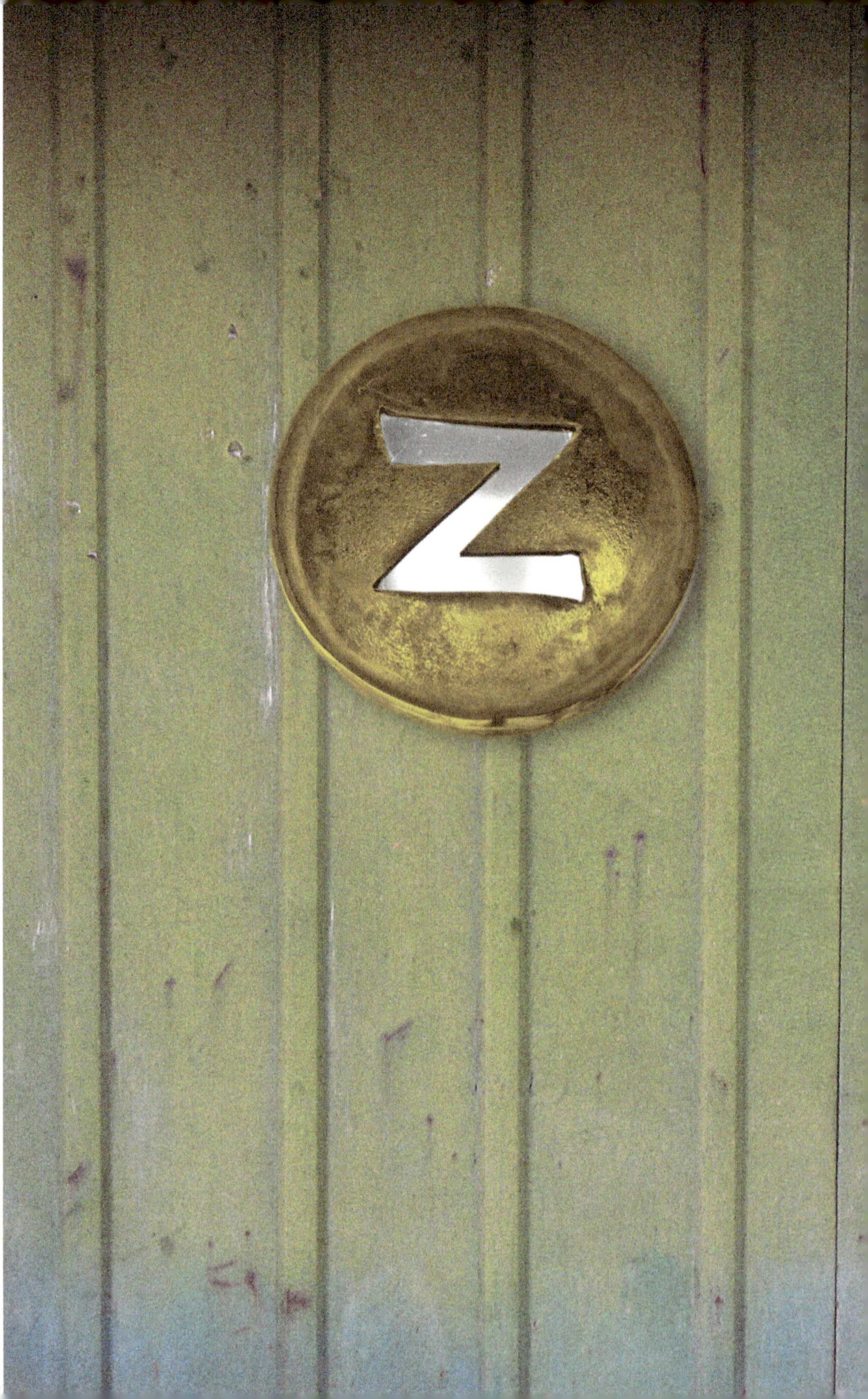
Z

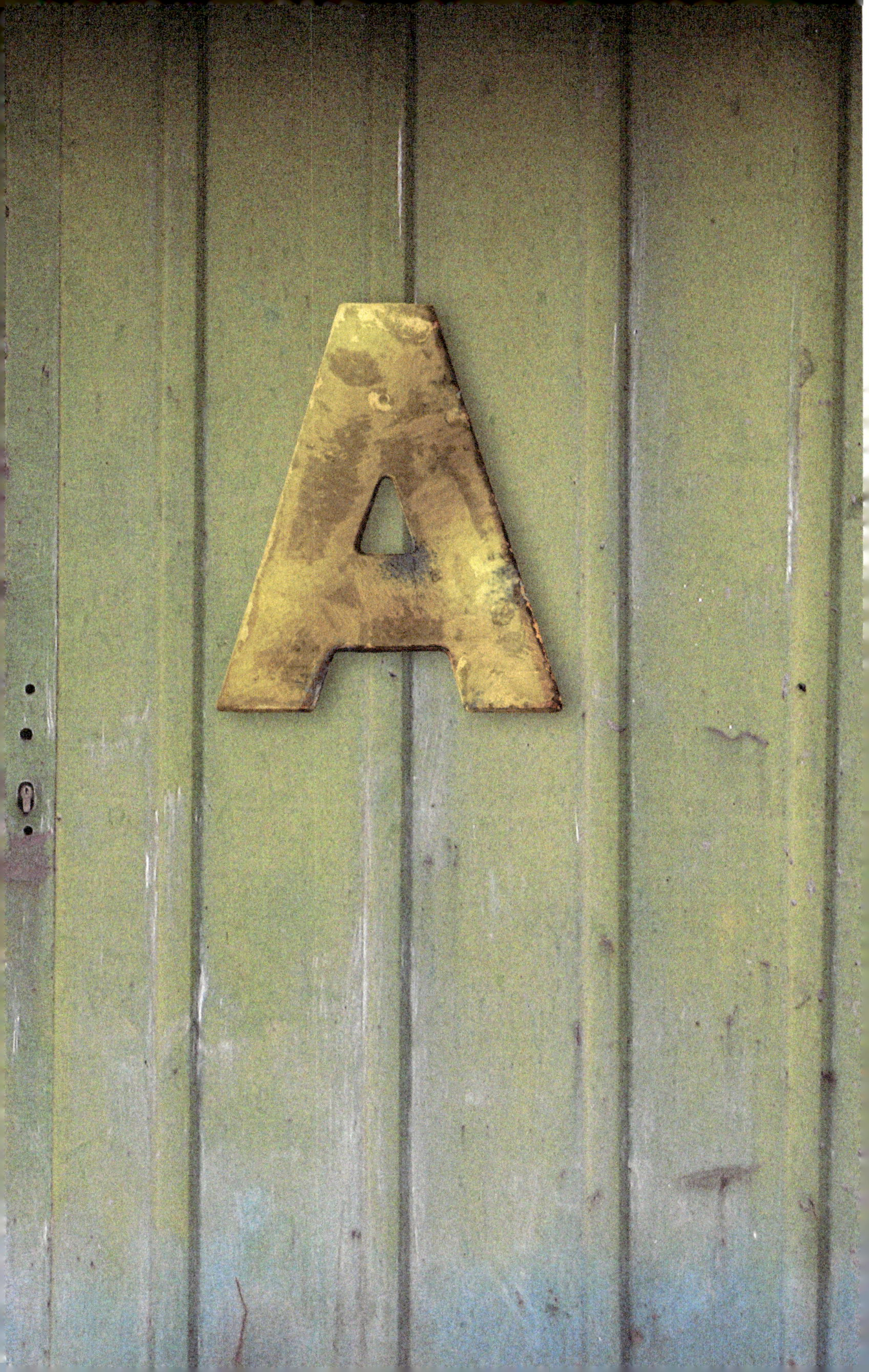
A

AFTERWORD

This book started in such a simple way. My friend Mark Winter had created an Alphabet of letters made of scrap metal and other junk-like objects. It was in an Art Show at a Chicago Art Gallery.

After the show, I had a vision of a junkyard with a tower of letters forming a word over the mountain of junk in the middle of the Junk Yard. I decided to create a story that began with a teen boy who is abandoned in the junkyard by his folks. He begins forming a word on the junkyard mountain as his own way to make contact with the world around him. The word was

a b a n d o n e d Z

Then, Abby, a girl his age, turns up asking about the tower of letters. Her idea is to change the letters on the junk mountain to "spell out" the Alphabet:

Z to A

Abby begins working with him and his dog, Moxie, on this new tower of alphabet letters.

Real life is around the writer all the time, and around mine came Susan Murphy-Milano, a national authority on domestic violence. We became friends and I learned "her story" which involved the death of her parents in domestic violence. I, like much of the world, didn't know much about domestic violence or its reach and grasp within our culture. I learned much from Susan and those who have shared their stories with me.

So, the world of domestic violence made its way into my

simple story of Abby, Zane and Moxie and the tower of letters. My reason for creating the story changed. Now, when people ask me why I wrote this story I tell them it's because I want to start a conversation.

Most of those who have read or been told this story have been sympathetic or know people whose lives have been badly touched and endangered by domestic violence. In particular, a dinner party in Florida where I met some new friends and told them about my story. The wife of a new friend left the room rather than commenting on the story. Later, she came back and sat with me and told me fragments of her story and ended up by putting her hand on mine and saying,

"I am glad you are writing this story — people need to know about this."

Others have voiced similar sentiments.

There have been, however, two or three who have said that they didn't feel right about my story in which a teen girl kills her father (in her mind, to save her mother's life) and, gets away with it. It is this part that they feel is morally wrong: the "getting away with it" part.

After thinking about this I realized that I wanted to start an argument about who should get away with what! That is, there is an enormous amount of damage, physical and emotional created by domestic violence. People are "getting away with it" every day— and some of the people I have met continue to suffer emotionally and in their personal psychology with the damage done to them as young people, to say nothing of the women who end up in Emergency Rooms all over the country with physical (and emotional) damage done by violent spouses. Yes, they are mostly men.

This book is dedicated to those people as well as my friend Susan Murphy-Milano, recently deceased, who inspired me to take the turns in the story I have taken. I admire her work in helping women everywhere to turn away from domestic violence and save themselves and their children from this stain that turns up in families more often than you would think... to bring it out in the sunlight for discussion and examination, and ultimately, to help to stop domestic violence.

I am grateful to you, the reader, for your willingness to read my book and give it some thought as well as see the marvelous invention of the letters of the alphabet by Mark Winter.